The Fables of
LA FONTAINE
Books I - VI

Newly translated by Pearl Hochstadt

Illustrations by Billy Wood

To Richard Howard,
In gratitude,
Pearl R. Hochstadt

⊙ iUniverse®

THE FABLES OF LA FONTAINE
BOOKS I - VI

iUniverse books may be ordered through booksellers or by contacting:

iUniverse
1663 Liberty Drive
Bloomington, IN 47403
www.iuniverse.com
1-800-Authors (1-800-288-4677)

Because of the dynamic nature of the Internet, any web addresses or
links contained in this book may have changed since publication and
may no longer be valid. The views expressed in this work are solely those
of the author and do not necessarily reflect the views of the publisher,
and the publisher hereby disclaims any responsibility for them.

Any people depicted in stock imagery provided by Thinkstock are models,
and such images are being used for illustrative purposes only.
Certain stock imagery © Thinkstock.

ISBN: 978-1-4917-7039-9 (sc)
ISBN: 978-1-4917-7040-5 (e)

Library of Congress Control Number: 2015910620

Print information available on the last page.

iUniverse rev. date: 08/05/2015

Book III

Contents

Book IV

Book V

Preface

Another Translation of the *Fables*:
Why? And How?

For over three hundred years the *Fables* of Jean de La Fontaine (1621-1695) have delighted French readers, captivated by their wit and charm. Indeed, memorizing the first few poems has long been a staple feature of a French child's early education. However, those who go on to examine the entire oeuvre—twelve books containing some 240 poems in all—soon recognize a mature sophistication that leaves the simple lessons of childhood far behind. One can find examples of fables stressing the importance of morally upright behavior, but far more common are those that embody worldly wisdom, the rueful recognition of the innate frailties and follies of humankind. So, like all proverbial wisdom, La Fontaine's "messages" are full of contradictions. Some advocate prudence; some celebrate boldness. Some praise generosity; others warn against the danger of showing generosity to treacherous types. But what unites all of them is the artfulness of their telling: the *poetry.*

La Fontaine did not invent his stories. With few exceptions, he took existing material, especially the fables attributed to the semi-mythical Greek slave Aesop, and gave it a fixed form, using the devices of traditional poetry—rhyme and meter—to compose versions that linger in the mind exactly as created. That's why former French schoolchildren can still recite the earliest poems well into old age. So can I, a fact that I mentioned in a poem written in 1998 on the occasion of my fiftieth-year high school reunion. That was when I first learned that he had written many more poems than the two I had been exposed to and enjoyed in French class. And that was when this translation project was launched.

Immediately I encountered the translator's unavoidable challenges. The Italians have a proverb, *Tradurre e tradire* (Translation is treason).

And it is true that the unique character of each language makes impossible demands. That is why there are so many different versions of such classic works as the epics of Homer or Dante's *Divine Comedy*—many excellent, all different, and all inevitably unable to capture every nuance of the poet's art. Eventually I framed the essential challenge as a negotiation or balancing act between the competing claims of the goddesses I called Fidelity and Felicity. Raw literal accuracy (if that were even possible) would sometimes have to yield to the demands of rhyme and metrical flow. Similarly, my efforts to approximate La Fontaine's frequently irregular metrical patterns would often have to be sacrificed to move the poem along. Compromise would always be necessary.

And why did I take up that challenge? "For fun" would be the most accurate answer. When I wrote that poem in 1998, I had already been retired for more than six years, and I was looking for a project that would occupy me until I reached the age of eighty. If I committed myself to translating just one book a year, I'd be right on schedule. And so I began. I faithfully maintained a pattern of devoting one hour a week to the task until I got to Book XII. Because it was more than twice as long as any preceding book, it required two hours a week and then a bit more time, but by 2011 the work was done.

As I plowed through the increasingly unfamiliar material, I was struck not just by its "timeless" wisdom but also by its topicality. The stage on which La Fontaine's animal surrogates enact their (read "our") business was not just personal but political, and there was hardly a current social or political issue on which our fabulist did not have something to say. His appreciation of *realpolitik,* developed and sharpened by his situation at the outskirts of the court of Louis XIV, is evident in many poems. When should one go to war? Consider the warning message of "The Lion" (Book XI, Fable 1). How should war be waged? See "The Dragon with Many Heads and the Dragon with Many Tails" (Book I, Fable 12). On a more immediate level, I could not help but see the relevance of "The Partners" (Book I, Fable 6) to circumstances in my own community, where powerful real estate interests were likely to get "the lion's share" from the sale of our local library. Still, some things do change. Decisions on matters of war and peace are no longer made by absolute monarchs. And, a "fable" in Book XI, "The Peasant from the Danube," actually anticipates and celebrates this change. (I put the word "fable" in quotation marks because the source of this poem is not an invented tale but real history, mentioned, La Fontaine notes, in the writings of Marcus Aurelius.)

Historical change is not the only change I discovered. Working my way through all twelve books, I also saw how La Fontaine's reach was extended and how his outlook evolved. Aesop would be supplemented by more obscure sources, such as the fifteenth-century Italian humanist Abstemius and the exotic Indian fabulist Pilpay (also known as Bidpai), and even, in the later books, by direct arguments with other contemporary thinkers. The most striking example comes at the end of Book IX in "Discourse Addressed to Mme. de La Sablière." There, La Fontaine explicitly disagrees with Descartes's contention that animals are mere programmed machines unable to think the way human beings do. He makes his case very convincingly, I think, citing numerous examples of adaptive behavior by a whole variety of creatures: stags and partridges and many others. But it certainly isn't a fable in the traditional sense. Similarly, Book XII moves even further away from the pithy sprightliness of the earlier fables to indulge in rambling reconstructions of tales from such classic works as Ovid's *Metamorphoses.*

My own attitude toward the project also evolved. What had begun as a pastime not very different from doing the Sunday *New York Times* crossword puzzle became an ambition. Francophone friends and knowledgeable poet/translators had given me positive feedback, and I had even had some of my shorter pieces published in *Metamorphoses: The journal of the five college faculty seminar on literary translation.* Eventually I recognized that I wanted to share my work with a larger public. Yes, I knew that well-regarded translations already existed, but I fortified my resolve by thinking of the examples of Homer and Dante and their many translators.

A trickier question was whether or not to publish a bilingual edition. I had made a point of trying to honor Fidelity as much as possible while still aspiring to meet Felicity's demands, but no one could evaluate that effort without seeing the original French version. Indeed, when I printed a small bilingual "sampler" of twenty-five representative poems, most of my readers appreciated the opportunity for comparison. In the end, though, I decided against it. And I even found support for my decision in one of my favorite poems, "The Miller, His Son, and the Ass" (Book III, Fable 1), in which the Miller, after receiving an unending stream of conflicting advice, decides "I will do as *I* please" (italics mine). Moreover, what pleased me now was supported by La Fontaine's own general nod of approval for practical realism, especially his acknowledgment of the reality of aging and mortality. Rather than wanting to stretch out the project, I was now in a hurry to finish, and preparing a bilingual edition would be just too difficult and time-consuming for this old lady to undertake.

But there would be a price to pay. The only way to understand my choice of many metrical irregularities would be to recognize that they were an attempt to approximate La Fontaine's own metrical choices. So here is my compromise. For those who care enough to want to compare my versions with the French originals, I recommend the purchase of the inexpensive *Classiques de Poche* edition that I used. The benefits of owning this book go far beyond that basic purpose. It is far more scholarly and thorough in providing background information about La Fontaine's life and times as well as his sources than anything I could reproduce. And some of its textual notes illuminate interpretive subtleties that I would otherwise not have registered. Indeed, I have occasionally allowed such information to creep into my text even though it can't be found in the original. A good example would be "The Fox and the Grapes" (Book III, Fable 11). Without the notes, I would not have known why La Fontaine had specified that the Fox was of Gascon or Norman origins. Three years of high-school French would never have given me a clue.

Another decision I had to make in preparing this volume was whether to make it comprehensive or selective. The quality of my translations was uneven—as indeed was the quality of the originals. An argument could be made for including only the best examples. But even though I had gone through the process of rating the poems on a scale from Poor to Very Good, when I looked over my notes I discovered that often the same poem had received a different rating during a different reading session. It would be easiest—and fastest— and most pleasing to my own vanity (that persistent human failing that La Fontaine so often acknowledged) to put my entire output on display. But even the vainest of us wants to highlight her best work, so I'd like to call my readers' attention to this list of the poems that I included in my Sampler:

Book I: 1—The Grasshopper and the Ant; 2—The Crow and the Fox; 3—The Frog and the Bull; 7—The Fault Collection; 20—The Cock and the Pearl

Book II: 1—To the Overly Critical; 3—The Wolf Accusing the Fox, with the Ape as Judge; 5—The Bat and the Two Weasels

Book III: 1—The Miller, His Son, and the Ass; 7—The Drunkard and His Wife; 10—The Lion Struck Down by a Man; 11—The Fox and the Grapes

Book IV: 1—The Lion in Love; 3—The Fly and the Ant; 5—The Donkey and the Little Dog; 7—The Ape and the Dolphin; 8—The Man and the Wooden Idol

Book V: 3—The Little Fish and the Fisherman; 7—The Satyr and the Traveler; 12—The Doctors; 14—The Donkey Carrying Relics

Book VI: 6—The Fox, the Ape, and the Animals; 11—The Donkey and His Masters; 12—The Sun and the Frogs; 16—The Horse and the Donkey.

Another compromise I chose to make is reflected in the above list as well as in the entire contents of this volume. Like La Fontaine, I have decided to issue my work in two volumes, with the first consisting of Books I through VI. These contain the liveliest, most delightful selections. Whether I will get around to publishing Books VII through XII remains to be seen. But once again I can find my justification in one of the fables, "The Little Fish and the Fisherman" (Book V, Fable 3), with its closing reminder, "No matter how small, what I've already got/Is certain. The future is not." Those who wish to encourage me—or offer any other advice—are invited to send their comments to my e-mail address, phochstadt33@gmail.com.

Acknowledgments

Over the long course of this project I have received generous help from Francophone friends who supplemented the limited knowledge of the French language I had acquired in high school. Thank you, Helene and Denise Andreu, Anne Barabasch Leyden, Jacqueline Verity (deceased) and, above all, Jenny Batlay, whose early and ongoing enthusiasm continues to sustain me. Thanks too to other friends who provided critical and technical support: Esther Goodman, Katherine Hogan, Laurie Lewis, Mira Stillman, and, chiefly, Ann Henry, who produced two precursors of this book and who also brought on board her friend Sarah White to provide the charming illustrations for my *La Fontaine Sampler.* Similarly, my good friend Vivian Levy deserves thanks for directing me to another talented artist, Billy Wood, whose illustrations enliven this book. Billy and Sarah have contributed so much to my project. My son, Jesse Hochstadt, also deserves heartiest thanks for guiding me through the tortuous paths of twenty-first century technology.

While I was still far from finished, I submitted some of my poems to *Metamorphoses*, a scholarly journal devoted to literary translation. Five poems: "The Frog and the Ox," "The Cock and the Pearl," "The Wolf Accusing the Fox, With the Ape as Judge," "The Satyr and the Traveler," and "The Doctors" were published in its Spring 2008 issue. And the editor, Thalia Pandiri, described my translations as "witty, modern, and faithful." I was also delighted when the distinguished poet/translator Richard Wilbur, to whom I had sent a sample of my work, described it as "admirable" and said I "stand up very well to the competition" and when his younger contemporary Richard Howard said that mine was a "fine, lively text which would give any new reader a sense of what La Fontaine is about."

The Two Mules

Book I

I The Grasshopper and the Ant

Miss Grasshopper, engaged in song
   All summer long,
With wonder found herself deprived
When the winter storms arrived.
Alas for her, she'd not put by
Even a speck of worm or fly.
"I'm hungry," was her plaintive chant
To her neighbor Mrs. Ant.
"Lend me just a bit of grain.
I will pay you back again
Completely and with interest too
Well before the loan is due.
I give my solemn creature's pledge."
Such language set Ant's teeth on edge.
This beggar took her for a friend!
(Besides, she didn't like to lend.)

"How did you earn your livelihood,"
She queried, "when the times were good?"
"In happier times I liked to sing.
You don't begrudge me such a thing?"
"You liked to sing? Well, good for you.
Now you can take up dancing too."

II The Crow and the Fox

Perched on a treetop, behold Master Crow
With his mouth crammed full of cheese.
Lured by the scent, Master Fox sits below
    And sounds him with pleasantries
"Greetings, M'lord" is his studied homage.
    "Aren't you the handsome fellow.
A voice to match such splendid plumage
    Must be both sweet and mellow.
    Cross my heart, you've got to be
    The height of vocal glory
    Deserving of celebrity
    Throughout this territory."

It works; the crow just has to show
    How gorgeous he can sound.
He shapes his mouth into an O.
    The cheese falls to the ground.
Fox seizes it and smirks, "Dear sir,
    Here's valuable advice.
To learn to distrust a flatterer
    A cheese is a trifling price."

Wracked with confusion, shame and pain,
    Crow views his sorry state
And vows he'll not be tricked again
        Just a bit too late.

III The Frog and the Ox

    A frog beheld a bull.
    It seemed a dandy size.
Under the spell of envy's pull
She thought, "By doing exercise
Huffing and puffing to swell my frame,
Perhaps in time I'd look the same."
No bigger than an egg was she
Yet such was her temerity
She bade her sister watch her grow.
"Am I there yet?"
          "Believe me, no."
"How about now?"
          "Not even close;
You're scarcely larger than at first."
So, filled with visions grandiose,
She strained until—surprise—she burst.

Poor wretch. And yet the world is full of folks who put on airs.
Petty officials dispatch underlings
To show the world they're men of great affairs.
Minor nobility dream of being kings.
Every merchant aspires to live like a lord
Though he bankrupt himself with a house he can't afford.

IV The Two Mules

Two mules were going down a country lane.
They bore quite different burdens on their backs.
One merely carried several sacks of grain,
The other silver for the royal tax.
The latter, glorying in in his grand commission,
Strutted, bells ajingle, head held high,
Proudly convinced that under no condition
Would he consent to set his burden by
When, out of nowhere, his astonished eyes
Saw, bearing down, an avaricious troop.
His precious charge their contemplated prize,
They caught his reins up with a sudden swoop.
In fighting back he took a mighty blow
        That made him groan and sigh,
"Surely it wasn't meant to happen so
That my companion safely passes by
        While I am left to die."

His comrade gravely answered, "Friend,
Lofty assignments don't guarantee enjoyment;
If you'd been in a miller's low employment
You wouldn't have come to such a sorry end."

V The Wolf and the Dog

A hungry wolf reduced to skin and bones
    So long as the watchdogs stood guard
Encountered once in unfamiliar zones
A mastiff who had wandered from his yard.
The fellow was so very sleek and fat
        The wolf would willingly
Have leapt on him and torn him limb from limb
        But for suspecting that
He'd met a foe too powerful for him
And therefore had to act with policy.
    So, speaking humbly by intent,
    He paid the dog a compliment,
Praising his plumpness and glossy fur.
    "Indeed, it's simple, my dear sir;
To be well fed like me is up to you,"
Replied the dog, "Here's all you have to do.
Just leave the woods, that god-forsaken hell
Where only stingy, starving wretches dwell,
Where one can never count on spitted meats
    Or other dainty proffered treats.
Follow me and you'll make out very well."

"Isn't there something else I'll have to do?"
"Practically nothing. Only to give chase
To beggars and ruffians who hang about the place,
Flatter the household and your master too
    And you'll receive all sorts of scraps
      That tumble from the feasters' laps
    Along with many a fond caress."
    The wolf was almost brought to tears
    Envisioning such happiness
Till he spied the sores behind the mastiff's ears.
"What's that?" he said.
              "Nothing."
                 "Nothing?" "Oh well, maybe
My collar made that little patch you see.

Rest assured, it doesn't bother me
And I don't even wear it all the time."

"What? You let a collar curb your liberty?
Your 'nothing' seems to me a major crime.
Not for your bill of fare, however nice,
Not for the world would I accept that price."
So saying, he ran off and still runs free.

VI The Partners

A heifer, a she-goat and a ewe once agreed
To band with the lion, the neighborhood boss.
The plan they envisioned to serve the group's need
Was to share with each other both profit and loss.
Soon after, the goat brought a deer that had drowned
In her lake to her partners to act on this plan
And the lion commenced, while the rest stood around,
To count on his paws; this is how the count ran.
"One, two, three, four. So four portions we'll make,"
Which he did and then added, while guarding the pot,
"As a Lion, of course, I'm entitled to take
Without question the very best piece of the lot."
The others stood dumbstruck. He reached in once more
Declaring, "This next piece is mine too by right,
The right, you must know, that accompanies might.
As for the third piece," his voice reached a roar,
"I claim that as well as the bravest in sight.
And if one of you dares think of touching piece four,
Make no mistake, she'll be killed on the spot."

VII The Fault Collection

Mighty Jove said one day, "Now let all of my creatures
To the feet of my grandeur draw comfortably near
So that, should they deplore any one of their features,
They may announce it without fear
        And I'll arrange a remedy.
Ape, you'll be first as you've the right to be.
Look at yourself and the rest of the lot;
Carefully study their graces and airs.
Are you satisfied?" "Yes," said the ape, "and why not?
My four legs are every bit equal to theirs.
When I look in the mirror, I like what I see,
A fully formed visage, unlike the poor bear's;
That's the kind of rough draft no one'd bother to paint."
Whereupon all expected to hear the bear's complaint
For his many defects. Instead he loudly boasted
And found himself faultless but heartily roasted
The elephant, sum of misguided design,
A shapeless grotesque one might barely refine
By cutting its ears off and stretching its tail.
The latter, in turn, showed its scorn for the whale.
Now there was a creature outlandish in scale!
And the ant put the flea down: "Too tiny by half
Yet it thinks it's a giant," she said with a laugh.
So Jove sent them all packing, all self-implicated
By the very contempt with which others were slated
While "perfection" described just how they should be rated.

Still, amidst all this folly it's notable that
Mankind is the species that beats all the others,
To his own imperfections as blind as a bat,
Sharp-eyed as a lynx when it comes to his brothers'.
Unlike the so-called lower orders,
Our scorn needn't cross zoological borders.

Since the dawn of creation we're somehow equipped
With a means of dividing folks' faults into two.
Our own out of sight are conveniently slipped
While those of our neighbors are left in plain view.

VIII The Swallow and the Little Birds

A swallow in her traveling
Through much observation had grown very wise.
        She noticed every little thing
And could forecast a storm from the least clouded skies
        Sharing her gift of prophecy
        With sailors on the bounding sea.

Now it chanced at the time that the hempseed was planted
That she spotted a peasant out sowing his field
And she rushed, with the horror her insight had granted,
To warn of the peril his harvest would yield.
"Little birds, I am worried and sorry for you
For the day of your doom is most surely at hand
Especially since you're unable to do
As I do and fly to some faraway land.
        I see devices to entrap you
        And other snares in which they'll wrap you.
        They're in the making, I foresee
        And promise death or slavery
        In time to come. Beware that fate,
        A birdcage or a dinner plate.
        Therefore," the swallow urged the birds,
        "Eat up these grain seeds, every one."
        Laughing, they mocked her warning words,
        "It's just too much; it can't be done."

        Later, when the fields turned green
        She tried again, "Pull up each sprout
        Of cursed grain or feel the keen
        Onslaught of doom, beyond a doubt."
        "Babbler, fearmonger," one bird spoke,
        "That's setting us a pretty task.
        To pluck the whole field as you ask
        We'd have to press some thousand folk."

When the hemp was fully grown
The swallow said, "It's looking bad.
A sorry time is coming soon
Though you wouldn't believe me. If you had
You'd see the farmers finally
Have got a respite from those chores
That kept them laboring outdoors.
Your turn is next, I guarantee.
The war is on, the snares are set.
Poor little birds, they'll get you yet
Unless you hide or imitate
The wildfowl—ducks, woodcocks and cranes,
Who don't sit still but emigrate
Traversing seas and desert plains,
An escape which, alas, you can't manage at all.
So you'd better just hide in a hole in the wall."

But no one would listen. She seemed in their view
Like the hapless Cassandra as mad as a hatter
And she'd only to utter her first word or two
To set them all off in a twittering chatter.
Like the Trojans of old, they too were enslaved
When by paying attention they could have been saved.

It's our curse to tune in only to our own fear
  And not see coming harm till it's already here.

IX The Town Mouse and the Country Mouse

Long ago, a mouse from town
With manners most polite
Asked his country cousin down
To share a tasty bite.

Ortolans were their dainty fare
On a Turkish carpet spread.
Imagine them just sitting there
Cozy and amply fed.

The meal they ate was surely grand
With not a thing amiss
Till something utterly unplanned
Chanced to disturb their bliss.

From just outside the door
Came a horrible sound.
Need I add any more?
Neither mouse stood his ground.

The noise being gone, "Time to retire,"
The country mouse said to his host.
"No rush. Let's sit around the fire
And finish up our roast."

"No sir," the country mouse replied.
"Tomorrow you will dine with me.
Granted, my cottage can't provide
Such elegance and luxury.

But nothing's going to spoil our night.
Intruding on our leisure.
Cousin, farewell. I scorn the pleasure
That fear can put to flight."

X The Wolf and the Lamb

That might equals right can be readily seen.
A little example will show what I mean.

    A lamb was gamboling one day
    In a sparkling mountain brook
When a famished wolf, driven to try his luck
In new surroundings, chanced to pass that way.
"What makes you so bold as to splash where I drink?"
    He swelled with anger. "Do you think
    I'll stand for such temerity?"
    "Please," said the lamb, "Your Majesty
    Has no cause to be vexed with me.
    I'm frolicking about, I know,
    But see, I'm twenty feet below
    Where you are standing. There's no way
    I'll roil your waters while I play."
    "I say you do," said his cruel foe,
"And furthermore you slandered me last year."
    "Impossible. I wasn't even here.
I'm so recently born I still suckle my mother."
"It wasn't you, then, but it could be your brother.
I can't make a fuss over who was to blame.
One of you did it. That makes *you* fair game.
I must have my revenge. I will brook no denial.
Don't count on your shepherd to come to your aid.
If he brings on his dogs, they will surely be beaten.
For I have been maligned. There's no need for a trial."
So saying, he rushed to a near forest glade
With the poor lamb in tow to be slaughtered and eaten.

XI The Man and His Image

A man all puffed up with a sense of his worth
Believed he'd no peer on the face of the earth.
He scorned as untrue what he saw in the mirror
And lived out his days quite content with his error.
To cure him, some meddlers determined to try
To always keep mirrors in front of his eye.
So they drew on the bluestockings' favorite device,
That silent conveyor of unwelcome advice,
With mirrors at home and mirrors in shops
And mirrors on garments of ladies and fops.

All in vain. Our Narcissus kept out of their way,
Seeking out remote spots where no mirrors held sway.
But these haunts were the site of so crystal a stream
As to make his escape an impossible scheme.
Though he hated the image these waters reflected,
Their beauty exerted a powerful force
That drew him repeatedly back to its source.
So, in spite of himself, his conceit was corrected.

My drift must be clear, but I'll make it more plain:
This man and his folly are hardly unique
For at heart we are all of us equally vain
And the mirrors of other folks' faults are too weak,
No matter how truly they show us our own,
To teach us the lessons we'd rather not know.
We need a pure source, one we face all alone,
Which we find in the *Maxims* of La Rochefoucauld.

XII The Dragon With Many Heads and the Dragon With Many Tails

An envoy of the Grand Seigneur
Sent to the Holy Roman Empire
Said that he rated his own lord's troops higher
Than his host's. This prompted a demur.
"Our prince's forces," he was told,
"Are led by men with so much gold
That each one can hire his very own army."

The envoy, being a man of sense,
Answered, "I've heard of the immense
Resources they command, but it doesn't alarm me.
Rather, it brings into my mind
A strange adventure that may well be true.
I was in a safe spot when there came into view
A hundred-headed Hydra, all its heads aligned.
My blood ran cold at such a sight;
I thought that I would die of fright.
Yet my fear was unfounded; no harm came my way.
Those multiple heads could not hold sway
Over the body nor put it into play.
I was pondering this strange affair
When another dragon with but a single head
Yet many a tail, all of them duly led
By that one chief, emerged from out its lair.
Again I was seized with amazement and fear
As the head passed by and the tails brought up the rear.
Nothing could impede their well-ranged powers.
And that, I hold, makes very clear
The difference between your emperor and ours."

XIII The Thieves and the Ass

Two thieves who had stolen an ass came to blows,
One wishing to keep it, one wanting it sold
But as they were pummeling ears, mouth, arms, nose,
They were foiled by a twist neither one had foretold;
       A third thief ended their dispute
       By seizing the contested loot.

Now the ass in this story's like some patch of land
    And the thieves are like this or that prince,
Not just two of them either, you must understand,
    But so many the thought makes me wince.
Turks, Transylvanians, Hungarians and more
    Fighting over the same bit of soil,
While, as they are squabbling, to settle the score,
    Some new thief makes off with their spoil.

XIV Simonides Saved by the Gods

There are three sorts of folk one cannot overpraise:
    One's mistress, one's king, and the gods.
Malherbe said it first, and I'll give any odds
    That his maxim's still good in these days.
So delighted are those whom our praise gratifies
That the hand of a beauty is often its prize
And the gods too have often rewarded it well
    As the poet Simonides found.
He'd once been so unwise as to promise to dwell
    On the claims of an athlete to glory
But his search for material struck barren ground;
    He just couldn't compose a good story.
Brute physical strength was his subject's sole merit.
From his commonplace parents he'd failed to inherit
    Even one trait that ought to be crowned.

Our poet picked through this unpromising stuff
    And did with it all he could do
Till frustration compelled him to cry out "Enough!
    I'll just have to try something new.
About Castor and Pollux there's plenty to write.
    I could keep at it day after day.
So distinguished were they when it came to a fight
    That I'll never lack something to say."
So he lauded their exploits, observed how their strength
Put them up with the *crème de la crème.*
The result was that fully two-thirds of the length
    Of his poem was devoted to them.

The athlete had promised to pay him quite well
But, seeing the finished production,
He gave just one-third and proceeded to spell
Out the grounds for this major reduction.
"Your praise of those twins was so lavish, you see,
I'm sure they'll come up with the rest of your fee.
    I'd like to treat you, all the same,

So come tonight and dine with me.
I promise you it won't be tame
And there'll be first-rate company.
My folks will be there and my dearest friends too.
To make it quite special, I'm counting on you."

Simonides promised, perhaps out of fear
He'd lose more than his fee if he chose to decline
Combined with the hope that perhaps he might hear
His own praises sung as they sat down to dine.
    He went and all went swimmingly
    Until a maid came running in
    Disturbing the festivity
    To tell him that two gentlemen
    Were at the door, full of insistence
    He come at once. So out he dashed.
    The others offered no resistance.
    To tell the truth, they all were smashed.
Surprise! The two men were the heavenly pair
Coming to thank him but also give warning:
If he valued his skin, he should flee then and there.
For the house wouldn't last till the following morning.

Their prediction came true; a column gave way,
The roof tumbled in and destroyed all the dishes
Not to mention their bearers. Indeed, I must say
That the ultimate damage was still more pernicious.
The vengeance they'd wrought was made wholly complete
When a girder fell, crushing the athlete host's feet
    And crippling almost all the others.
    So potent were those angry brothers.

All through the town the story soon spread.
    "A miracle!" the people said.
    "That poet's fees must surely double
    For whom the gods would take such trouble.
    Only a churl of ignoble birth
Could fail to see what such connections are worth."

18

To return to my theme, let me simply repeat
There are those for whom praise cannot be too replete,
The gods above all, but the Muses as well
Who, without condescending, permit us to sell
The fruit of our labors, receiving their due
When those that we praise likewise honor us too.
    As they win glory, we earn gold
For Parnassus and Olympus are friends from of old.

XV Death and the Malcontent

An unhappy wretch spent all his breath
   In constant sighs to Death.
"Oh, Death, you seem so beautiful to me.
Come quickly now and end my misery."
"I might as well oblige him," Death once thought.
She knocked at his door, entered, and showed her face.
"What's this I see?" he cried out, overwrought.
"Remove this horror to some far off place.
Death, you're more hideous than I can say,
More scary too. Oh Death, please go away."

   Maecenas was a gallant chap.
He said somewhere "If I should lose my hand,
Be crippled, suffer impotence or gout
Or any other terrible mishap,
Without a single qualm I'd stick it out
Happy to be alive. I'd have Death banned
Forever; all men would, I have no doubt."

XVI Death and the Woodcutter

A poor old woodcutter bent under the load
Not just of his faggots but also his years
Dragged himself onward with groaning and tears
As he struggled to reach his pathetic abode.
At last, overcome by his grim twofold weight,
He set down his burden and mused on his fate.
Had he known any joy from the time of his birth?
Could there be one more crushed on the face of the earth?
Often hungry and always unable to rest,
Beholden to creditors, children and wife,
By taxes, forced labor, and soldiers oppressed,
He surely had led a most miserable life.

   He called on Death. She came in a trice
   And asked him how she could
   Be helpful. "Could you be so nice
   As to shift this load of wood?
   I know you're ready to bring relief
   But we're not so ready to die."
   Faced with oblivion, we'll bear our griel
   That's the creed all men live by.

XVII The Middle-Aged Man and His Two Mistresses

A middle-aged man
At that point in his life
When grey hairs just began
Thought of taking a wife.
Since his income was good
　　As things stood
There were plenty of women determined to further his views
By trying to please him and win him however they could
While he, for his part, was not in a hurry to choose
　　In a matter of no trivial import.

Two widows, among all who paid him court,
Attracted him, one young, one more advanced
　　In age, but mistress of the sort
　　　　Of arts by which each handsome feature
　　　　Is skillfully enhanced
While playing down the ravages of nature.
Both of them had a favorite sport.
Laughing and joking, they'd play with his hair
　　But each with a different aim.
The first plucked any white hairs she found there;
　　The other's version of this game
Was pulling out the black ones so his pate
Would better match that widow's present state.
In time these tricks, it scarcely need be said,
Left him without a hair upon his head.
The end result? He thanked them heartily
　　And didn't begrudge the cost.
　　"I've gained more than I've lost
By learning married life is not for me.
In entering this blissful state (so-called)
　　I'd be the one plucked bald
　　To suit another's style
I'm grateful for a lesson so worthwhile."

XVIII The Fox and the Stork

Grandpa Fox once asked to dine
His old acquaintance Granny Stork
But costly fare was not his line;
He barely owned a knife and fork.
A poor thin soup was all the food
Presented by this arch cheapskate
And in a manner still more rude
He served it in a single plate.
Ere his guest's long bill could take a drop
The rascal lapped its contents up.

Seeking revenge for this shabby trick
The stork asked him to be her guest.
"Why sure I'll come. No need to stick
To fancy forms when the request
Comes from a good old friend like you."
The date was set. He hurried to
His hostess' home prepared to praise
The well-cooked meat—and then to graze.
He sniffed its scent with appreciation
For "Good appetite" is a fox's vocation.
But when she brought the banquet out
He blushed to see its presentation.
A long-necked vase, no pouring spout,
The narrow hole on top served well
For the entry of Dame Stork's long bill;
His muzzle's malapropos design
Deprived him of any chance to dine.
Crestfallen, tail between his legs,
His stomach growling, full of shame,
He slunk back to his sorry digs
And who but himself was there to blame?

Reader, if trickery's your game,
My tale has found its proper aim.

XIX The Child and the Schoolmaster

This fable's intended to make very plain
How foolish and vain many critics can be.
It starts when a schoolboy fell into the Seine
And might well have drowned were it not for a tree,
A willow whose branches, thank Heaven, he grasped.
"Someone save me. I'm drowning," he frantically gasped.

Now a schoolmaster happened to be passing by
And he turned and looked grave when he heard the boy's cry.
This boy needs a lesson, he firmly decided.
"You impudent monkey, just see what you've done.
How your parents must suffer, expecting," he chided,
"The grief that awaits such a rascally son.
I pity them both, and I warn others too
To beware of the likes of a knave such a you."
So his lecture proceeded full ten minutes more
Till he finally pulled the poor schoolboy ashore.

> But to me the one who's most to blame
> Is the sort who likes to play the game
> Of scolding, preaching, babbling on.
> You know the type. They're often found
> Occupying places in the sun,
> Flooding their hearers with the sound
> They love the best—their own tongue's wagging,
> Not caring that someone may have drowned
> Before their flow of words starts flagging.

Say, friends, come first to give me help.
    Afterwards you're free to yelp.

XX The Cock and the Pearl

Finding a pearl in the road one day
A rooster carried it away
To one who sold such things.
"I'm sure it's very fine," said he
"But it offers less delight to me
Than a single oat grain brings."

Bequeathed the *Works* of a noted poet
An ignoramus rushed to show it
To one who sold such things.
"No doubt," said he, "it's worth a lot
But I'm just as happy if I've got
What a single penny brings."

XXI The Hornets and the Honeybees

A worker's deeds announce his name
As the Honeycomb Saga makes known.
Some hornets claimed it for their own.
    Some bees opposed their claim.
The case was brought before a wasp
And proved too subtle for him to grasp
For the witnesses' sworn testimony
All agreed that the ones who'd made the honey
Were winged, buzzing, brownish creatures.
Alas, both species shared these features.

Puzzled, the wasp decided that he
Had better extend his inquiry.
He went to an anthill to find an adviser
And emerged from its precincts none the wiser.
Till at last a sensible bee protested;
"It's absurd how long this has been contested.
We've been at it six months and in all of that time
We've not pinned down a single fact
And the honey's gone bad—now that's a real crime.
It's time the judge improved his act.
Forget these silly cross examinations,
These counter-charges and obfuscations.
Just let both parties set to work
To show that they know how to build
Such honeycombs. We bees won't shirk
The task. You hornets, are you skilled
Enough to prove your claim that way?"
The hornets refused. The case was closed.

Would that every trial could be disposed
By such applications of common sense.
It would save the litigants much expense

As well as emotional wear and tear.
As it is, when it's settled they're nearly dead
And the measly awards are rarely fair
And only the lawyers come out ahead.

XXII The Oak and the Reed

The oak one day said to the reed
"Nature has treated you shabbily indeed.
Should even a kinglet choose to alight
Among your leaves, you would feel its weight
And the faintest breeze, one so very slight
As merely to ripple the water's face,
Would bow you down, while in my case,
    A build as sturdy as a rock
Not only shades the ambient space
But even defies the tempest's shock.
To me it's all zephyrs; to you it's all blasts.
Still, could you but grow where my foliage casts
Its sheltering shade, you'd be safe I've no doubt
And the fiercest of storms wouldn't knock you about.
Unfortunately, Nature's compelled you to grow
In swampy terrain where the stormy winds blow.
You've a right to complain."
                    But the reed shook its head.
"Your good-natured pity's uncalled for," it said.
"The winds are less threatening to me than to you,
For I bend and don't break. And while so far your strength
Has resisted their blows, what will happen at length
Remains to be seen. The conclusion's still due."

Even as it was speaking these words, there came forth
From the distant horizon a furious gale,
The fiercest wind ever to swoop from the North,
Leaving nothing but ruin in the wake of its trail.
    The reed bowed down. The oak stood fast.
    The storm came with redoubled force.
    The oak's proud posture couldn't last.
    Its roots, which once had intercourse
    With Stygian depths, were ripped away
    From earth's caress. Its lofty crown
    Which had kissed the heavens in its day
        Shuddered and toppled down.

The Astrologer Who Fell Into a Well

Book II

I To the Overly Critical

Blest perhaps at my birth by the glorious Muse
With those gifts she bestows on her true devotees,
For the theme of my verses I vowed I would use
The fictions of Aesop, aware of the ease
With which feigning and poetry happily consort.
But I scarcely believed myself gifted enough
To do more than engage in the fanciful sport
Of embroidering his tales with my own home-made stuff
Attempting, through rhyme, to embellish their matter.
(Let those who believe themselves wiser do better.)
Meanwhile, I'd contrived to make animals speak
In a new tongue, not just the original Greek,
Not just animals either, but flowers and trees
Gained voices, a feat I imagined would please.

        "True enough," my critics granted,
        "We have found ourselves enchanted
        By some half-dozen nursery stories."
Sneering praise meant to suggest that the glories
Of a higher style, more authenticity
Are quite beyond me. Well now, let us see:

"After ten years of war on the outskirts of Troy,
After hundreds of battles, a thousand assaults,
Countless stratagems, all of them riddled with faults,
The wearied Achaeans had yet to employ
A plan to assure that proud city's defeat
When Minerva decided to come to their aid,
Introducing among them a strange new device,
A wooden horse so marvelously made,

31

So huge its hollow innards could suffice
To hold whole squadrons and their leaders too:
The wise Ulysses, valiant Diomede,
Impetuous Ajax, a determined crew
Which, once inside Troy's wall, with all due speed
And unleashed fury, doomed its very gods,
A plan unheard of, beating all the odds,
Paying its makers for their dogged labor. . ."

"Enough," exclaimed a literary neighbor.
"These windy spoutings leave me out of breath.
Besides, your tale of armies bringing death
Sprung from a wooden horse is even more strange
Than that unlikely Fox and Crow exchange.
Aside from which, high style is not your line."

"All right, I'll sink a bit: Hark to the pin-
ing notes exhaled by lovesick Amaryllis
Mooning for her Alcippus yet full of fear
That none but sheep and loyal dogs would hear
The anxious sighs that issued from her jealous
Breast, aimed at Zephyr, but carried to the ear
Of Tircis as he glided through the willows . . ."

           "Stop right there," my critic howls.
           "I can't accept these feeble rhymes.
           Why, you haven't even matched your vowels.
           You'll have to rework this some dozen times."

           Damn carpers, can't you just keep still?
               I know quite well what I'm about
           And trying to please you is too uphill
               A task when all you do is pout.
You fussy folk are doomed to discontent.
You can't be satisfied; at last that's evident.

II The Rats' Council

A certain cat named Rodilard
Among the rats inspired such dread
If they but heard him breathing hard
They knew they were as good as dead.
So the few that escaped kept themselves out of sight
Even though it meant starving, so great was their fright.
As their stock of food dwindled to one half-bare shelf
Rodilard seemed to them like the devil himself.

Now it happened one day that the cat went abroad
Courting a lady cat. Here was their chance,
A singular respite which might just afford
Time to huddle together and try to advance
    A sorely needed plan of self-defense.

The Dean of Rats, well-known for his good sense,
Taking the floor, expressed his firm belief
That there was just one way to find relief.
Around the cat's neck they must put a bell,
Right away too. And then they all could tell
When once his deadly forays had begun,
Giving his victims ample time to run.
"That's what we have to do," they all agreed.
"You've found the one solution that we need."

But now the group discussion reached stage two.
Who'd undertake the job they had to do?
Suddenly reservations put to rout
Their early mood of triumph as they saw
Risk was involved—the project's fatal flaw.
"I'm not that crazy"; "You can count me out."
So nothing got done, an end I've often seen

When not just rats but other groups convene.
       When talk's involved the meeting hums
       Speakers and fine ideas abound.
       But when the time for action comes,
       Surprise, there's nobody around.

III The Wolf Accusing the Fox, With the Ape as Judge

Declaring he'd been robbed, a wolf accused
His low-life neighbor, Fox, and brought his suit
Before an ape, who found himself bemused
When each side claimed that it was the abused
And injured party. Judging this dispute
Would be, he saw, a taxing task indeed,
For both, rejecting lawyers, urged their case
With such fierce anger flaming in each face
That, in a sweat, Ape recognized the need
To tread with care where lack of evidence
Was covered up by vocal vehemence,
Charges and countercharges flung about
Until the partisans were both worn out.

Whereon Ape said, "My friends, for many years
I've known you and your mode of operation
And based on that, it certainly appears
That both of you must make full reparation,
Wolf, for your empty claims that can't be proved,
Fox, for the goods you've stealthily removed.
What other judgment could be fair and square
When one must deal with such a sorry pair?"

IV The Two Bulls and the Frog

Two bulls once were fighting over which would possess
        A heifer and the lands that came with her.
        A little frog sighed to see this mess,
        Setting her friends in a dither.
"What's the matter?" her fellow croakers exclaimed.
        "Why, can't you see," said she,
"What the certain result of this quarrel will be
        When one wins and the other is maimed?
        The bull who has been forced to yield
        Will have to leave his flowery field.
        Driven to exile, he'll seek some place
        Where he can reign despite disgrace
        And that will be our swamp, I fear.
        Think what he'll do by coming here.
        Trampling about, a brute that size
        Will squash us like so many pies
        All for the loss of Dame Heifer's eyes."

        Her fears proved only too well founded,
        For when the beaten bull had fled
        Into their swamp, his great hooves pounded
        And quickly crushed some twenty dead.
        Alas, it's always been the fate
Of small folk to pay for the follies of the great.

V The Bat and the Two Weasels

A bat by mistake poked her head in the nest
Of a weasel who, seeing her, thought, "That's a mouse,
        A creature who is such a pest
        I'm glad she's landed in my house."
Rushing to eat the poor thing, she declared
"You've got some nerve. Well, aren't you scared
Seeing that your race has plagued mine all these years?
Get ready to die. You're a mouse, are you not,
As sure as I'm a weasel."
                        "Oh no, you have got
        The wrong impression, it appears.
What? Me a mouse? Someone's been telling you lies.
        Thanks to the Maker of earth and skies
        I am a bird. Behold my wings.
        Long life, say I, to soaring things!"

        Her claim prevailed; it seemed so right.
        Released, relieved, the bat took flight.
        Yet after just a day or two
        With giddy heedlessness she flew
        Into another weasel's den,
        Her life in peril once again.
        What could she do when now she heard
        She would be eaten as a bird?
        Her wits revived. She brusquely said
        "Who put such notions in your head?
        If birds are your sworn enemy
        Then you've no cause to lunge at me.
        What makes a bird? Feathers of course.
        I am a mouse. Long live the rats!
        Let Jupiter confound all cats!"
        And so, by this adroit recourse,
        She once more gained her liberty.

So it is. Those who know how to doctor their shape
Or their colors can frequently make their escape,
Exclaiming according to how the wind blows
"Long live the king!" "Long live his foes!"

VI The Bird Wounded with an Arrow

Mortally struck by an arrow, a bird
Just before it expired pathetically stirred
To lament the cruel fate that compounded its woe
Making feathers the means by which it was laid low.
"Cruel humans, unfazed by the ugly intent
That takes our own wings for our death's instrument,
Your mockery rings hollow. Just look and you'll see
How often you're served just as badly as we.
Among Adam's descendants, one half of the brothers
Are keen to take up arms against the others."

VII The Bitch and Her Mate

As she approached the time to whelp,
A bitch in need of a sheltered spot
To rear her litter turned for help
To her mate and begged for the loan of his cot.
Hearing her pleas, he thought it best
To consent to such a modest request.
But when he returned in a little while
To reclaim his bed and his domicile
He was told he must wait a few weeks longer:
She couldn't leave till the pups were stronger.

The two weeks up, he returned once more
Only to find her blocking the door,
Baring her teeth with a snarling threat
While her pups stood round her, strong and stout.
They weren't ready to leave just yet:
"We'll go when you're able to push us out."

Helping wicked folk always is cause for regret.
They'll take whatever they can get.
If you expect to claim your rights
Be prepared for nasty fights.
Let them get just one foot in at your door
In no time they'll have planted four.

VIII The Eagle and the Horn Beetle

Lady Eagle gave chase once to poor Johnny Hare,
Who was running as fast as he could to his lair
When he spotted a horn beetle's hole on the way,
      Not much of a refuge need I say.
But he scrunched himself down, having no other choice
And the eagle prepared to make off with her prey
      When she heard a protesting voice.

"Princess of Birds, we both know you've the power,"
The horn beetle piped up, "both to seize and devour
My unfortunate friend. But I beg you, forbear.
He's a neighbor who's put himself under my care.
Don't dishonor the haven he's found in my cell.
If you carry him off, you must take me as well."

Disdaining to answer, she knocked him aside
With one blow of her wings. He stood silent and dazed.
He watched Johnny taking his lifetime's last ride,
Then, suddenly furious, he rushed like one crazed
To the aerie within which were proudly displayed
Eagle's dearest possession, the eggs she had laid,
The eggs that she cherished in hope they would be
In the fullness of time her beloved progeny,
And he smashed them to bits, sparing not even one.

When the eagle returned and saw what he had done
Her grief stricken cries through the heavens resounded
And her feelings of outrage were only compounded
By the thought that she lacked any means to get back
At the one who'd committed this stealthy attack.
Childless all through that year, she must suffer her pain
Resolving to build her nest higher next time,
Which she did, but the horn beetle managed to climb
Even there. Johnny Hare was avenged once again.

Her new grief caused the woods to ring
A full six months with her laments.
At last she went to see the king
Of gods, her patron ever since
She'd brought him his dear Ganymede.
Now he must help her in her time of need.
Into his lap she laid another clutch
Of eggs, convinced that none would dare to touch
Anything guarded by his majesty.
Correct. This called for a new strategy.
The beetle dropped some dung on the royal gown.
Brushing it off, Jove let the eggs crash down.

When the eagle found out
She started to shout
Shrieking at Jove, How dare he spill her pets?
He'd better hide—the mildest of her threats.
Poor Jove was dumbstruck. Then a new surprise:
Beetle appeared and launched into a long
Account of how that bird had done him wrong.
She disagreed. They couldn't compromise.

Jove pondered long and finally declared
He'd found a way to end this messy spat.
The eagle's brood would certainly be spared
By altering her breeding time so that
Her eggs would hatch in winter when the race
Of beetles hibernated, in which case
The rascal couldn't even show his face.

IX The Lion and the Gnat

"Get away, you vile pest, worst of all things that fly"
      Were the words that a lion once spat
      At a creature who plagued him—a gnat.
      "This means war," was the gnat's quick reply.
"Do you think I am scared by that crown on your head?
      Do you think that I shake at the knees?
An ox is much stronger than you are," he said
      "Yet I drive him about as I please."

      Whereon he gave his battle cry
      As both trumpeter and chief
      While sizing up the means whereby
      He best could bring to grief
      His haughty foe, then dived straight for
      The lion's neck—and made him roar.
His eyes flashing anger, the half-crazed beast
Caused his neighbors to scatter in two seconds flat,
Their wholesale terror caused by the least
      Of creatures, a measly gnat,
Who had meanwhile found lots of new points of attack,
Striking now at his muzzle and now at his back
      Now causing his nostrils to itch.

The lion's rage had now reached such a pitch
His tiny nemesis just laughed to see
How every exposed spot was made to twitch,
How tooth and claw struck back so frantically
He only bled the more. His tail lashed out
And struck his flanks. In ever-mounting fits
He beat the harmless air and whirled about
Until exhaustion made him call it quits.

The gnat left the field at the height of his glory,
His trumpet triumphant proclaiming his story
To all who would hear, But, alas for our friend,

A spider's ambush laid him low
And he too met his end.

What lessons does this story show?
First of all, when it comes to assessing our foes
The most to be feared may be smallest of all.
Also, though one escapes the most dangerous blows,
A trifle may cause one's downfall.

X The Ass Loaded with Sponges and the Ass Loaded with Salt

A donkey driver, staff in hand
Borne like a scepter, proudly led
Two long-eared steeds, his to command.
One, who was bearing sponges, strode ahead
    Swift as a courier while his mate
    Just dragged himself along, the weight
Of bags of salt no small impediment.
So, loaded thus, our merry pilgrims went
O'er hill and dale, their progress only stayed
    When they arrived upon the shore
Of a broad stream. It seemed they'd have to wade,
Something the driver'd often done before.

Mounting the ass who was carrying sponges,
He prodded the other ahead with his pole.
The beast lost his footing and took a plunge. His
    Bags sank with him into a hole.
He floundered about and then up he heaved.
    The water had dissolved the salt.
    Of his heavy burden now relieved,
To the opposite bank he could easily vault.

Whereon Comrade Spongebearer, as meek as a sheep,
Blindly followed his lead and plunged into the deep.
Ass, driver, and sponges were all held down
    Because of the water those last took on,
    Not only sharing but causing their fate.
All three drowned on account of that added weight.
The donkey struggled with might and main;
The driver clung to him, prepared to die.
Someone tried to rescue them—all in vain.

There's a moral in this, very sad but true;
There's often more to lose than to gain
    By acting just as others do.

XI The Lion and the Rat
XII The Dove and the Ant

One must try to help others whenever one can.
Even tiny folk often can come to one's aid.
The two fables that follow make patently plain
      How often these truths are displayed.

      Up from between a lion's paws
A rat crept toward the light, bedazed and in confusion.
The king of all the animals made use of this occasion
      To demonstrate how generous he was.
    He spared it. Now just think of that
      A Lion caring for a Rat!

      But the story continues from there.
As the kindhearted lion was leaving the wood
      He found himself caught in a snare.
Though he roared out in anger it did him no good.
Then the rat he had spared rushed to pay back his debt.
With patient persistence he gnawed through the net.
      The little chap achieved at length
      Results not gained by rage or strength.

The next tale involves creatures tinier still,
A dove and an ant; the first drank from a rill
When she spotted the latter, who'd just tumbled down
Into the current and likely to drown.
As it struggled in vain to get back on dry land
The dove, out of charity, came to its aid.
She tossed it a grass blade, which luckily spanned
The distance to shore. So the rescue was made.

By chance at that moment a barefoot lad came
Bearing a crossbow and looking for game.
He spotted the dove and his mind raced ahead

To the feast he'd enjoy once the poor bird was dead.
But just as the villain prepared to take aim
      The ant bit him hard on the heel.
He swiveled around to see who was to blame,
Time enough for the dove to observe and take flight
      Carrying off the lad's coveted meal.
      He'd have no bird for supper that night.

XIII The Astrologer Who Fell Into a Well

Have you heard how one day an astrologer fell
As he gazed at the stars to the foot of a well?
The poor devil whose feet scarcely knew where to tread
Still believed he could read what he saw overhead.

There's a lesson in this from which others may learn
For his is a folly that many folk share.
Though they dwell down on earth they look up at the air
       Convinced that there they can discern
       Exactly what will come to be
As inscribed in the Book that they call Destiny.
But this book of which Homer and others have told,
What is it but Chance, as they called it of old,
       Or what we now call Providence?
And Chance can not be known to prescience
       For if it were, 'twould surely not
       Be known as Chance, Fortune, or Lot,
       All things defying our prediction.

As for the Will who gives our lives direction
       Who but Himself is privy to the plan
That's doubtless in His mind but which we cannot scan?
Why would He use the stars as text at night
When darkness often veils them from our sight?
What purpose would it serve? Well, maybe mental sport
For geometric wits and others of that sort?
To help us to avoid evils we can't prevent?
To substitute for joy eternal discontent?
Since pleasures known too soon too often lose their savor,
Foreknowledge, I maintain, would scarcely be a favor.

It's more than just an error; in fact it is a crime
To fasten on such notions. Instead, let us observe
The wheeling heavens' path: The stars don't ever swerve.
       Daily the Sun begins its climb.
Daily its brilliant passage obliterates the dark

Without demanding from us any profound remark.
So far from the unveiling of mysteries occult,
The message of its motion is regularity.
Season succeeds on season. The predictable result:
Crops ripen, bodies are heated, and eyes begin to see
A pattern one can count on, its inevitable advance
Completely unrelated to the vagaries of chance.

You charlatans who ply us with us with your horoscopic charts,
It's time you packed your baggage and lit out for other parts,
And take with you those alchemists still hoping to convince
With their hocus-pocus theories some naive untutored prince.
But I'm getting too excited. It's sufficient to turn back
And recall once more the tale of that infatuated hack
Whose folly sent him tumbling, whereby we can observe
How vanity metes out the fate its followers deserve.
    If they're the only victims, fair enough.
Let them just not hoodwink others with such stuff.

XIV The Hare and the Frogs

A hare lay brooding in its lair
(What better place for brooding if one must think at all?)
When he found himself plunged into deepest despair,
Beset by the terrors that held him in thrall.
          "We timid souls live in such dread
          That misery's our lot," he said.
"No pleasure's untainted. We're always assailed.
There is scarcely a crumb we can swallow in peace.
Just see how I live. Due to terror," he wailed
"I don't even dare close my eyes when I sleep
And the clever advice 'Just stop worrying's cheap
          When fear itself inhibits fear's release,
          I bet I'd find on inquiry
          Even humans are afraid like me."
Such were the thoughts that made him fret.
          Despite his care to be on guard
          Anxiety kept him breathing hard.
A sigh, a shadow, anything—or nothing—made him sweat.

          While thus reviewing all his fears
          And groaning at his wretched lot
He heard a faint sound and he pricked up his cars.
"Danger!" he shrieked and he fled like a shot.
He passed by the edge of a pond in his flight
Where frogs leaped about and then dove down below.
Was his presence the reason they scurried off so?
          Could he have caused their fright?
"My goodness," he thought, "they're reacting to me
As I would react to some huge enemy.
          Their panic boggles all belief.
          They take me for a warrior chief.
Let a chap be fainthearted as ever he will
He's bound to find someone more fainthearted still."

XV The Rooster and the Fox

Keeping watch from his perch in a branch of a tree
      A wily old rooster espied
A fox who declared in tones sweet as could be
      "Let us put our old quarrels aside.
I've hurried to say this because I'm about
      To embark on a very long trip.
So please don't delay. Quick, before I set out
      Let's acknowledge our new fellowship.
From now on you and yours will have nothing to fear,
      I will cherish you just like a brother.
      The time for making friends is here,
      So come down from your perch, my dear
      And let us embrace one another."

"My friend," the bird answered, "You couldn't have brought
      A message more welcome and sweet
          Than this
          View of bliss
And my rapture is still more complete
In that you are the messenger. I'm quite overwrought.
And see, down the road here come two sturdy hounds
Rushing to join us by leaps and by bounds.
Sent to spread this glad news, they are making their rounds.
I'm sure that's their aim. They are coming apace.
I'll descend now and that way we all can embrace."

"Oh dear," said the fox, "I am sorry to say
I have so far to travel I just cannot stay.
      We'll have to make it another day."
      And in no time flat he was on his way
      Shaking with panic and disgust.
      His clever scheme had been a bust.
      Meanwhile the rooster laughed at his flight.
      To outfox a fox is a double delight.

XVI The Crow Who Wanted to
Imitate the Eagle

A crow saw an eagle descend in mid flight
       To snatch up a sheep on the wing
And though nowhere as strong he'd as much appetite
       And resolved he would do the same thing.
He studied the flock and at last fixed his eyes
On the finest and fattest, a veritable prize,
       A sheep the very gods might wish
       To find before them on a dish.

The crow spoke up brightly while tenderly gazing
At this beauty, "I don't know who reared you thus far
But my compliments to her. You're so above par
       That I'm sure you'll make excellent grazing."
So saying, he pounced on his scared would-be prey
Whose unrestrained bleating proclaimed her dismay
And who weighed (need I say it?) far more than a cheese,
Far more than his slight frame could carry with ease
While her thick curly fleece (Cyclops' beard was no thicker)
So entangled his claws it was he who was trapped
Till the shepherd came running and seized him, and quicker
Than you can say "boo," the poor fellow was clapped
Into a birdcage to serve as a pet.

There's a lesson in this: One must never forget
That size makes a difference. A poor petty thief
Is out of his depths as a grand robber chief.
Imitation is tricky. Appearance deceives.
Moreover, despite our most cherished belief
Success sometimes comes to the tiniest thieves.

XVII The Peacock Who Complained to Juno

A peacock addressed a complaint
To his patroness Juno, declaring
"I have certainly cause to lament
For my voice, thanks to you, is so blaring
And screechy that only a saint
Could endure it, while anyone hearing
The song of that miserable mite,
The nightingale, gets a real treat
From a voice that's both brilliant and sweet
And is ravished with utter delight."

Full of anger, the goddess replied
"How dare you indulge in such spite
As to envy the nightingale's voice
When I've decked you with features so choice
That you ought to be swelling with pride?
A neck like a rainbow, a bright
Sweeping fan of a tail all bedight
With highlights that sparkle and gleam
Like a jeweler's extravagant scheme.
What bird is more gorgeous to view,
More splendid and pleasing than you?

"I would never bestow all my gifts on one creature
Giving each one instead a particular feature.
Some have grandeur and force meted out as their portion;
The falcon is swift and the eagle is brave.
The crow utters warnings that urge men to caution.
The raven's predictions are even more grave.
Not one's discontent with the voice that I gave.
Just keep up your whining, but the price that you'll pay
Is I'll snatch your fine feathers away."

XVIII The Cat Who Turned Into a Woman

A man once so doted upon his dear kitty
He called her his darling, so dainty and pretty.
    Her purring notes would make him drool.
    You couldn't find a greater fool.
    In his infatuated love
    He cried out to the gods above,
    Went in for magic spells and charms
    And, lo, one day found in his arms
    A maiden (who had been his cat)
    And married her upon the spot.

    His amorous folly reached such heights
    He swelled with ecstasy and pride,
    Finding the sum of all delights
    Embodied in his brand-new bride.
    He'd tickle her, she'd stroke his face.
    His self-deception saw no trace
    Of any trait that wasn't human.
    To him she was the perfect woman.

    Then suddenly their fond embrace,
    The pleasures of the marriage bed
    Were troubled by a band of mice
    Who came and nibbled on the spread.
    Madame ex-cat did not think twice.
    She leapt on them; away they fled.
    But some came back, failing to see
    The features of their enemy.
    She pounced again. Her change in looks
    Had not extended to her nature.
    For Nature's a force which blithely mocks
    All efforts to reform a creature.
    It shapes behavior in a mold
    That's fixed before one's very old.
    After that one tries in vain
    To alter its accustomed train.

Beating and prodding won't do the trick
Even if one wields a heavy stick.
However one tries to be the master
It's bound to end up in disaster.
Slam the door on an unwelcome face;
Watch it pop up in another place.

XIX The Lion and the Ass Out Hunting

To celebrate his birthday, the king of all the beasts
      Decided to go hunting—and in style.
He planned on prey befitting this most glorious of feasts.
Sparrows wouldn't do; they'd scarcely be worthwhile.
      He had much grander objects in his mind,
Fine bucks and boars and stags and others of that kind.

      Seeking success in his endeavor
      He realized it would be clever
      To enlist the service of the Ass,
      Calling upon his voice of brass
      To be his mighty hunting horn.
      So he hid the Ass in a heap of boughs
      And gave the signal for him to bray
      Knowing the beast had not been born
      Whom that Stentor's blast would not arouse
      To freeze in terror and then dash away.
      Out from their homes all the forest folk fled
      Only inevitably to be led
      Into the trap that had been prepared.
      They rushed on blindly and down they fell
      Into a pit and were ensnared.

      "Your Majesty, haven't I served you well
      On this occasion?" the Ass declared,
      Taking full credit for the hunt's success.
      "Indeed," said the Lion, "I have no doubt
      If I were a creature who hadn't found out
      The disposition of you and your race
      I'd be every bit as unduly scared."

Had he dared, the poor Ass would have countered the slight
With indignant expressions of anger and scorn
But the Lion had taken his measure aright.
What Ass has the courage to blow his own horn?

XX Aesop Construes a Will

If all that they say about Aesop is true
    His genius was unparalleled.
    His insight penetrated through
    Legal conundrums which had held
    Entire law courts in a state
    Of paralyzed perplexity
    Undone by their complexity,
    A point that I can illustrate
    With a charming tale I'll now relate.

    A father had three daughters who
    Could not have been more different.
    One was a flirt, one liked her brew,
    One couldn't bear to spend a cent.
    The local law code specified
    That his last will and testament
    Must treat the daughters equally
    So when the time came to divide
    The inheritance, each of the three
    Got one-third of his property.
    But to this dictate of the laws
    He'd added a peculiar clause.
    Their mother, too, must get her share
    Payable when each had spent
    Her portion. But what would then be there?

    The father died. The daughters sped
    To the chambers where the will was read,
    Trying to make sense of what it said.
Lawyers were consulted. They studied the will
Reviewing its language from every angle.
They rummaged for precedent cases until
They finally judged it a hopeless tangle.
The only approach they could recommend
Was to split the estate and to ask the heirs
    Voluntarily to extend

A pledge that one-third of what was theirs
Would go to their mother on demand
(Assuming she'd take such a guarantee
      Instead of an annuity).

      Agreed. Three lots were soon created
      Each having its own character
      And to the first were designated
      The land and goods one might prefer
      If food and drink were one's chief joys:
      Vineyards and vessels and serving boys,
      Pavilions for inviting friends
      To share the pleasures of gourmands.
      The second lot had all the things
      A flirt might crave: fine furnishings,
      A town house, costly robes and rings
      And servants who would slave away
      To put their mistress on display.
      The third lot had the farms and fields,
      The flocks and folk whose labor yields
      A tidy profit sure to please
      A lover of economies.

      The parceling out was called inspired.
      Each girl would get what she desired.
      Only Aesop was unmoved.
      He told folk why he disapproved.
      "For all their labors and their pains
      Those lawyers," he told them, "lack the brains
      To recognize the true intent
      Of the deceased's last testament.
      Were he alive, I have no doubt
      He'd scorn the way they've worked things out
      Marveling that men who seemed so shrewd,
      Who gloried in their subtlety
      Should have so badly misconstrued
      The aims behind his will's decree.
      Now, leave the parceling out to me."

So saying, he took the portions back
And started on a different tack.
In line with Aesop's clever scheme
Each got the lot she'd least esteem.
The miser got the fripperies
Dear to the heart of the coquette,
Whose share comprised all that would please
A member of the drinking set.
The lush's lot those barns and leas
Her thrifty sister longed to get.

The settlement that he advised
Made sense because he recognized
There was no surer guarantee
That each would sell her property.
And once they'd turned it into gold
The benefits would be twofold.
With cash on hand, they'd have to act
As their late father wished them to
And pay their mother her full due.
Their money also would attract
Men from the finest families
Who valued handsome doweries.
Amazed, folk faced the stunning fact:
"Just think that one man's piercing mind
Saw more than all of us combined."

The Lion Struck Down By a Man

Book III

I The Miller, His Son, and the Ass

Since artistic invention dawned ages ago
We must honor our forebears the Greeks, yet I know
That the fields where they labored haven't been picked so clean
That we latecomers cannot find something to glean.
In the country of fiction we still can explore
And discover terrain left unplotted before.
Observe, for example, this nicely turned piece
That Malherbe told Racan—and it didn't come from Greece.

These two rivals of Horace, the heirs of his lyre—
No, their gifts from Apollo must place them much higher—
These masters, I say, on occasion once met
As they often did privately (these têtes-à-têtes
Affording them freedom to safely confide
Those thoughts and concerns they might otherwise hide).
Racan took the lead, "Friend, please help me decide
As someone much older and wiser," he sighed,
"Who knows so much more about life than I do,
What sort of profession I ought to pursue.
Shall I move to the country or settle at court
Or go for a soldier? That might be fine sport.
All the world is a mixture of pains and delights.
Even war has its pleasures and marriage its frights.
If I followed my own tastes I'd know what to do
But I've so many others to satisfy too,
My dependents, the court—I must please the whole lot."

"Please them all?" laughed Malherbe. "Then you're sure on the spot.
But before I advise you, please let me regale
Your ears with the following interesting tale.

61

It's a tale I once read and recall that it had
As its principal actors a strapping young lad,
His father—a miller, and one more as well,
The family ass, which they wanted to sell.
They planned to see what it would fetch at the fair
And to increase its value decided to bear
The beast on their shoulders so when they got there
He'd be fresh as a daisy, spared all wear and tear.

"Like some grand votive offering they bore him aloft,
Poor, ignorant simpletons. 'Have they gone soft
In the head?' roared an onlooker choking with laughter.
'What game are they playing? They couldn't be dafter.
As sure as I stand here, this spectacle shows
That the biggest ass isn't the one you'd suppose.'
Upon hearing these words the poor miller turned red
With chagrin. 'We must change our positions,' he said.
'Let the beast do the walking and, Son, you can ride.'
Though the donkey complained, the boy gladly complied.

"So they went on their way till they happened to pass
Some merchants who, seeing the lad on the ass,
Expressed their displeasure; 'This never will do.
That a graybeard should wait on a stripling like you
Is unthinkable. Get down at once,' they all cried.
'It's your role to follow while he mounts astride.'
'If that's what will please you, then that will be done,'
Said the miller, exchanging his place with his son.

"But now three girls passed by and the first of them said
'It's disgraceful to see how that old fool is led
With the grand self-assurance a bishop might claim
While that boy limps along. What a miserable shame.'
'I'm not quite the ninny you think,' he shot back.
'I've a right . . .' But the lasses kept up their attack.
The taunts flew back and forth till, admitting defeat,
He shifted his weight and created a seat
For his son. The poor donkey now carried them both
And he'd scarcely gone thirty more steps on his path

When new critics appeared. 'Are those madmen?' they said.
'They've so loaded their beast that he soon will be dead.
Or are they so cruel that they simply don't care
And are planning to barter his skin at the fair?'

"'By God,' said the miller, 'one can surely go mad
From the effort to please the whole world—and its dad.
Still let's try one last time ere we come into town
To have done with this matter.' Whereon both got down
Allowing the ass to trot gaily ahead
Till they met someone else. 'I'm astonished,' he said.
'Is this the new fashion, to let donkeys prance
While their owners' discomfort is not worth a glance?
Who's supposed to be tired, the beast or its master?
Keep it up and I forecast you'll meet with disaster
As that song about Nicholas courting his Jeanne
Reminds us. When spurned, he departed the scene
Riding off backwards, to face certain death,
A donkey like you two—but why waste my breath?'

"'That's it. I'm convinced, I'm a donkey, OK?
But from now on no matter what others may say
If they blame or refrain, if they wish me in hell,
I will do as I please.' And he did—and did well.

"As for you, follow Mars, follow Love, or our King.
Come or go or stay put. You can do anything.
Take a wife or take vows. Take a job, take a walk.
There's one thing I'm sure about. People will talk."

II The Limbs and the Stomach

It well may be that Royalty
Has been the prompter of my art
And given it the shape you see
By taking on the Stomach's part.
If that has any needs, the whole body's on call.
Legs, arms, fingers and hands, how it wearies them all.

So one day they resolved they would follow its lead
And be equally idle. Like gentlefolk they
Would not sweat any longer, no longer obey.
"Without our hard labor let's see how he'll feed.
We do all the work and get none of the gains.
It's that belly alone who's enriched by our pains.
His lesson of indolence we'll willingly learn."
Their words led to deeds—or, to be more exact,
To non-deeds as each of the rebels in turn
Stopped working. The fingers abandoned the act
Of picking up food, the arms drooped, and the feet
Stood still as they challenged the Stomach to eat.

All too quickly they realized their foolish mistake.
They too soon were starving; they too had a stake
In the Stomach's well-being. They'd thought him a sloth
And discovered his functioning profited both
Himself and themselves. Truly, more than the rest
He gave the whole body its vigor and zest.
And to Royalty's grandeur the same thing applies.
It both gives and receives and the gain equals out.
Though all work to support it, they too have their prize,
Obtaining the food they cannot live without.
The craftsman's endeavors receive their reward;
The merchant's enriched and the judge has his pay;
The laborer, the soldier, each one in his way
Is maintained by the grace of their sovereign lord
 Who sustains the whole State 'neath his sway.

Menenius in Rome had the same thing to say
When he watched as the Populace grumbled and swore
That the power, the riches, the honor, the fame
        All went to the Senate, while they
Felt the burden of taxes, the travails of war.
The Senate was worthless; they'd go their own way.
They'd clear out of town. That would fix their foe's game.
They were right at the gate when Menenius showed
By means of this fable their status as Limbs
Who needed a center and, rebuking their whims,
        Led them back to the duty they owed.

III The Wolf Disguised as a Shepherd

A wolf gazing down at the mouth-watering sight
      Of some sheep who were grazing below
Thought deception might best serve his roused appetite;
      He'd adopt a new look head to toe.
So he dressed as a shepherd; he put on a smock
      And fashioned a crook from a stick,
Not forgetting some bagpipes to sling on his back
      As the finishing touch to his trick.
All caught up in his makeup, the wonder is that
He didn't write "Shepherd, That's Me" on his hat.

Thus disguised, with his shepherd's crook clutched in his paws,
He proceeded on tiptoe the better to peep.
There lay the real shepherd sprawled on the grass,
      Serenely, profoundly asleep.
His dog and his own pipes were fast asleep too,
      So likewise were most of the sheep.
He needn't disturb them, our hypocrite knew;
      He would just lure the rest to his lair.
But for that he must speak, clothes alone wouldn't do
      And that's how he botched the affair.
For his voice didn't sound like the shepherd's at all.
The whole forest reechoed when he started to bawl.

      Sheep, dog, and shepherd all awoke
      The moment that imposter "spoke."
      To make things worse, his shepherd's smock
      So tripped him up he found that he
      Could neither fight nor turn and flee.

Rogues always entrap themselves, thinking they're smart.
      If you're a wolf, stick to that part
      Or pay out dearly for your art.

IV The Frogs Who Demanded a King

        Grown weary and bored
        With democracy's sway,
        The frogs once implored
      "Jove, can't we try some other way?"

He silenced their clamor by sending on down
A king all equipped with a robe and a crown,
A gentle and peaceful king from Heaven's own height
But the noise he made falling created such fright
        Among those silly timid frogs
        That instantly they all took flight,
        Hiding deep under the reedy bogs,
        Not even daring to peek at the face
Of the giant who'd suddenly crashed through their space.

        Now that giant in fact was just a log,
        Weighty indeed but so still and mute
        That finally, tremblingly, one small frog
        Crept closer. Another one followed suit
        And then still another, then more until
        The swarm resembled a great ant hill.
        From moment to moment growing bolder,
        They jumped about on their monarch's shoulder
        Without provoking the least complaint.
        Their king was as meek as the meekest saint.

This was not what they wanted. Their dissatisfaction
        Led them to pester Jove once again;
"Please give us a king who can take some action."
"Very well," said Jove, and he sent them a crane
Who crunched them and munched them and gobbled them raw.
        The desperate frogs voiced a new protest.
        "Hold on," said Jove, "Is there any law
        That compels me to act at your behest?
        It's a pity that you weren't content

To appreciate self-government.
Having switched, how foolish to complain
Of the mildness of your first king's reign.
Be satisfied now lest you get
A new king who will prove worse yet."

V The Fox and the Billy Goat

Captain Fox went out walking along with his chum,
Friend Billy Goat, famed for his horns' splendid growth
But not for his wits; he was pitifully dumb
While the fox had been playing sly tricks since his youth.
Feeling suddenly thirsty, they plunged down a well
       And drank up the very last drop.
"That feels better," said Fox, "but, my friend, do pray tell
       Me how we can get back on top.
Well, I've got an idea. Lift your forefeet up high
       And lean your horns into the wall.
Then I'll climb on your back and your horns and thereby
       I'll get out of here first of all.
       And the very next thing that I'll do
       Is reach down and pull you out too."

"I declare," said the goat, "that's a wonderful plan.
       I could never in all of my days
Have figured it out. Minds like yours, though, who can
       Are certainly worthy of praise."

So the fox made his exit and then was so kind
As to preach to the victim that he'd left behind,
Urging patience and chiding, "Too bad that your sense
Isn't anywhere close to your beard's excellence.
If you had any brains you would not be so quick
To jump down a well. Now I've got to be going.
Try to get out somehow. While I wish you good luck
I must be on my way. There are things that need doing."

       The moral's clear: We need to see
When starting something what the end may be.

VI The Eagle, the Sow, and the Cat

An eagle kept its nurslings in the hollow of a tree,
        A sow's at the base, a cat's between somewhere,
A convenient separation which allowed each family
        To raise its youngsters as its own affair
        Till Cat's deceit destroyed it totally.

She climbed up to the eagle and she said to her "Beware!
Our doom—rather our babies' (but to mothers that would be
The selfsame thing)—is coming soon. You'd best take care.
Look down; observe the actions of that accursed sow.
She keeps rooting at the tree base and so weakening its frame
That it's bound to topple over. Our poor innocents, I vow,
        Will be the victims of her nasty game.
        Once the tree falls, you mark my words,
        She'll gobble up your baby birds,
My kittens too, but I'm thinking of you," the thrust of her dissembling.
With a farewell pat, the wicked cat left Mother Eagle trembling.

        She dropped in next
        With the same pretext
On the sow (who was in labor)
And whispered softly "Dearest friend and neighbor,
I've come to warn you of the harm you face
From Madam Eagle should you leave your place.
She's planning to swoop down and snatch your litter
But please don't breathe a word of what I say.
To her—or else my own lot will be bitter."
Her poison planted, Cat went on her way.

Now neither neighbor dared to venture out.
Their fear had made them foolishly forget
The basic fact, too obvious to doubt:
Their infants' need for nurture must be met.
Frozen in fear, all they could do was fret.
The eagle worried that the tree might fall,
Sow lest her babes be snatched up one and all.

What followed from this senseless consternation?
Both families were wiped out by starvation.
Not all was lost though. After they were dead
The family of cats was quite well fed.

What woes a treacherous tongue can weave
　　　Using its vile arts to deceive.
　　　Of Pandora's whole horde
　　　Of released forms of grief,
　　　By common accord
　　　The most justly abhorred
　　　Is a lying sneak thief.

VII The Drunkard and His Wife

We all have some faults that we just cannot shake,
      Swayed neither by shame nor by terror.
An old tale I remember serves aptly to make
This point—that no matter how grave the mistake
      We stubbornly cling to our error.
In this case the cause was a penchant for drink
      Pursued with no thought of the cost.
In no time at all, ere an eyelid could blink,
Our devotee of Bacchus was swept past the brink;
      Health, money and wits—all were lost.

One day when his bouts with the bottle went on
So thoroughly all of his senses were gone
His wife shut him up in the depths of a tomb
Where, gradually waking, he stared through the gloom
And the fumes still befuddling his liquor-filled head
At the various trappings surrounding the dead,
Shrouds and tapers and such. "What has happened?" he said.
"Can it be that I've crossed past the threshold of life
And now have a widow instead of a wife?"

Whereon she appeared in a Fury's disguise
And, masking her voice and averting her eyes,
Approached him and held out a steaming hot bowl
Suggestive of Lucifer, brimstone, and coal.
Convinced to the depths of his none-too-deep soul
That he was in Hell, he piped up, "Who are you?"
"Satan's cellarer," she groaned, "and I'm here to provide
Food for those sent to dwell with him after they've died."
      Without missing a beat her mate replied
            "But don't you serve drinks too?"

VIII The Gout and the Spider

When Hades created those plagues of mankind,
The gout and the spider, "My daughters," he said,
    "No doubt you will be proud to find
      Man views you both with equal dread.
But now it's time for you to choose by lot
Your dwelling place on earth. I have in mind
Two different sites. One of them's quite refined,
A gilded palace splendidly designed.
      The other one's a humble cot."

Winning the draw, Spider at once selected
The royal palace, as you'd have expected.
"Who wants to live in yonder wretched shack?"
Her perverse sister took another tack.
"Mansions are full of doctors," fretted Gout.
"If they ganged up on me, they'd throw me out."
She chose the other lot and settled down
In the big toe of a poor countryman,
Saying "There's work enough here to be sure
And not a sign of doctors, so I can
Sit tight nor fear they'll oust me with a cure."

Spider, meanwhile, assuming that she'd be
A resident for life, began to spin
A web amid the mansion's tracery
And very soon had lured two victims in.
At once a servant came into the room
And swept away her network with a broom.
She spun again. Again the broom came out
Putting both Spider and her web to rout.

Day after day she saw her work undone.
Defeated, she went off in search of Gout
And found her sister also on the run
And a thousand times more miserable indeed
Than any spider. Driven by her host,

73

She was hurried off to dig, to plant, to weed,
To chop up firewood. Half-dead almost,
"I can't go on," she said. "I need a rest.
Sister, let's just change places." Spider agreed
And gladly settled in that humble nest
Where brooms were never wielded, where her spinning
Would not require each day a new beginning.
Miss Gout in turn sped off and came to lodge
With a fat prelate, causing him such pain
An endless course of poultices proved vain
        And from his bed he couldn't budge.
        Gout never had to stir again.

Well, so it goes. Thinking that we know best,
How often do we only make things worse.
Yet now and then with common sense we're blessed.
We change our lodgings and escape their curse.

IX The Wolf and the Stork

With the outsized appetite
Of his race, a wolf once fed
So greedily he might
Any minute now be dead,
For a bone he had swallowed was lodged in his throat.
But he was in luck though he couldn't cry out
For just at that moment along came a stork.
        He signaled her. She ran to his aid.
With the skill of a surgeon, she set to work.
She pulled out the bone and then asked to be paid.

"You expect to be paid? You must be joking.
Consider, madam, what you have done.
How many creatures would, after poking
About in my throat, have emerged with their own?
Ingrate, be off. Think of Nature's laws
        And don't ever fall beneath my paws."

X The Lion Struck Down By a Man

Displayed in a gallery show
Was a painting that drew much applause
For in it a hunter laid low,
Unafraid of its huge fearsome jaws,
A lion much larger than he.
One lone hunter! Imagine folks' glee.
A real lion hearing their crowing
Observed "Yes, you like what you see
But the artist's deceived you, well knowing
He had just let his fancy run free.
Far from crowing, they'd sooner have cause to lament
If ever lions learned to paint.

XI The Fox and the Grapes

A fox who hailed from Gascony—or Normandy perhaps
(Both of them home to poseurs)—chanced to spot some luscious
grapes.
        Now he was nearly dead of hunger
        But the grapes, though rosy, were out of reach.
        He stared at them a little longer
        Then shrugged them off with an airy speech.
        "Who'd bother with grapes that aren't ripe?"
        Better (was it?) to feign disdain than gripe.

XII The Swan and the Cook

Within a private zoo
Well stocked with fowl were two,
A swan and a gosling who
Had each been assigned to a separate role.
The swan's was to delight
His master's sense of sight,
The goose his appetite.
And each was well pleased with his lot on the whole,
One a guest in the garden, one welcomed inside,
While both shared a moat where together they'd glide.
Together they'd plunge through the watery spray;
Together they'd surface and swim side by side,
Their competitive preening on frequent display.

Now one day when the cook had had one drink too many
In his fuddled condition he made a mistake.
Unable to tell which was goose, which was swan, he
Grabbed hold of the latter and throttled his neck
To make goose soup. His victim let out a faint cry.
Surprised, the cook cried "That's no goose,
Not with that voice," and let him loose.
"Had I caused such a beautiful singer to die,
God forbid, I could not look myself in the eye."

Life's full of danger, goodness knows,
But sweet talk may disarm our foes.

XIII The Wolves and the Sheep

After warring against them for thousands of years
The wolves told the sheep they were ready for peace,
For, they shrewdly observed, should hostilities cease
Both parties would profit, both cast off their fears.
Once they no longer fed on a sheep who might stray
In turn they no longer need scurry away
When a shepherd, enraged by the loss to his flock,
Set out to acquire a new wolf-skin smock.
       A formal treaty would provide
       Freedom to roam for either side.

"Agreed," said the sheep. But to make things secure
A clause was put in that was meant to insure
Their mutual safety: each party'd arrange
For a properly monitored hostage exchange.
The wolves gave their offspring; the sheep sent their dogs
(The terms duly inscribed in the monitors' logs).

Time passed. Soon the young wolves were babies no longer
And their taste for ferocity grew ever stronger.
But so did their wiles, and they bided their time
Till the shepherds were absent. Then, ravenous with hunger,
They pounced on the fattest young lambs in the fold
And carried them off from the scene of the crime
To the woods where their kin, who'd already been told
       In secret of their treacherous scheme,
       Had compounded their perfidy.
       While their unsuspecting charges slept,
       They stealthily approached, then leapt
       Upon the dogs so suddenly
       These had no time to turn and flee
       Or even feel what had been done
       But were torn to pieces every one.

So what should our conclusion be?
Against the wicked there's no recourse
But war, addressing force with force.
That peace is lovely we all agree,
But all of its charms might as well be dust
With an enemy you cannot trust.

XIV The Lion Grown Old

     The lion, once feared far and wide,
Wept the loss of his prowess as age took its toll
So harshly his subjects now boldly defied
     Their old sovereign, reversing their role.
The horse came and dealt him a powerful kick,
The wolf dared to bite, and the ox gored his side.
The miserable lion, enfeebled and sick,
     Couldn't even roar out, though he tried.

So he made up his mind to be stoic and suffer
When he spotted an ass coming up to his cave.
"Enough," said he. "I'm ready to go to my grave
But to bear this one's blows is to meet death twice over."

XV Philomel and Procne

Lady Procne, the Swallow, one day
Left her dwelling and flitted away
From the city where crowds of men dwell
To the depths of the woods, home of poor Philomel.
"Dear sister," she said, "how are you getting on?
Why it's almost a thousand years since you've been gone.
Am I right in recalling you've not shown your face
Amid human haunts since the old days in Thrace?
Think harder about how you live, I entreat.
Won't you ever depart from this lonely retreat?"
"Ah," said Philomel then, "Is your own life more sweet?"

Procne answered, "But blessed with so lovely a voice,
How can you justify making the choice
To bless only beasts with your beautiful song
Or the odd swain whom chance might send ambling along?
Such talents as yours go to waste in the wild.
Their splendor should shine in the cities, dear child.
Besides, I should think the unvarying sight
Of these woods would perpetually call up the fright
That you felt when King Tereus, his passions white-hot,
Raped you long years ago in a similar spot."

"That cruel memory lingers, you're right,
But that's just why I'll never go back,
For in looking at humans, alack,
The thought of how one did me ill
Would make memory's pangs fiercer still."

XVI The Drowned Woman

I am not one of those who say "Pay it no mind;
       It's only a woman who's drowned."
For unlike those scoffers, I know womankind
Is the source of such joys as the male sex has found
In our sojourn on earth. And you'll see that this fact
       Bears directly upon the sad case
Of a woman whom chance or some desperate act
Led to forfeit her life in the river's strong race
Which carried her off without leaving a trace.
  Her stricken spouse searched high and low
  Vowing that should he come upon her
  He'd give his loss its proper due
       And bury her with honor.

Now by chance some men were strolling near
The spot where she had fallen in.
"Excuse me, sirs, since you have been
Upon these banks, have you noticed here
A woman now vanished from the scene?"

"I'm sorry, I haven't," one man replied
"But why don't you search further down?"
"No," said his friend, "I bet if you tried
To go upstream you'd soon come upon
Her body because, as you very well know,
Female perversity must carry the day
And no matter the course that the stream tends to flow
  She'll proceed just the opposite way."

A tactless remark, even setting aside
The question of whether his view
Of the nature of women might be justified,
      A question I won't go into.
But one thing I do know: Whoever's inclined

At birth to enjoy contradiction
Will continue to keep that perverse state of mind
All his life as a constant affliction
       And not stop there but misbehave
       From cussedness beyond the grave.

XVII The Weasel in the Granary

Miss Weasel, whose body was slender and lithe,
Slipped into a granary through a small hole
   And at first was quite blithe.
   All the food that she stole
   Was abundant and free
   And she packed it all in,
Unaware as she downed it so ravenously
Of her swelling pot belly and new double chin.

At the end of a week she was startled to hear
A strange noise and decided she'd best disappear.
She tried to escape through the very same hole
But she just couldn't make it; she'd eaten too well.
"Have I made a mistake? Was it some other spot?"
She searched high and low, but of course it was not.
"It was here. But how strange, for I certainly know
That I fit through this hole just a few days ago."

Observing her struggles, a plain-spoken rat
Unriddled the puzzle. "Then you weren't quite so fat.
Being thin when you entered, you must exit as thin.
That's advice that some others might also take in."

But let's not make too much of this little affair
Or assume there's a lesson for us hidden there.

XVIII The Cat and One Old Rat

I once read in a fabulist's story
Of a cat who compared in his conqueror's glory
To Attila himself, Alexander the Great,
Or the famed Rodilard whose attacks sealed the fate
Of hundreds, nay thousands. But this cat's ambition
Went further by far, for he took as his mission
The goal of destroying all mice everywhere.
For miles all around he created such fear
Mousetraps seemed jokes compared to him.
        But his reputation had its price.
        His prey became so scared of him
        That soon he couldn't find any mice.

        Not daring to venture beyond their holes,
        Locked up like prisoners, these timid souls
        Were at least beyond the reach of his paws
        And therefore safe from his terrible jaws.
        Clearly he needed to hatch a plot
        That would lure his victims to venture out.
"I'll play dead," he decided, and in no time flat
        The mice beheld their arch-enemy Cat
        Suspended limply from a beam
And were taken in utterly by his scheme.

"He's been hanged for some crime," the mouse folk gloated,
"Stealing or scratching or damaging stuff.
Well, he got what was coming," they piously noted
"And we'll dance at his funeral, sure enough."
So, smirking and preening, they practiced their dance,
First a prudent retreat then a tiptoe advance.
        Emboldened they drew near—and then
        The cat could grab them once again.
He fell on those laggards who were the least
Practiced at running and had him a feast.

"The war's on again, and you'd better believe,"
He declared, "that I've more than one trick up my sleeve.
Your deep holes won't save you. The time will come
        When you'll be drawn into my home."
        And he was right. With a new device
        The rascal managed to fool them twice.
Covered with flour and crouched in a bin—
Such a simple disguise—but it took them in.
Not nimble enough for a timely retreat,
They crept up to their doom on slow, pattering feet.

One old rat alone was immune to this ruse.
He'd fought many a campaign and he'd learned at some cost
That by being foolhardy a soldier might lose
Much more than his tail (which he'd already lost).
So from a safe distance he loudly declared
"Don't think I'm back here just because I am scared.
I know that yon floury lump can conceal
A trap. And I don't intend making your meal.
You could pass for a statue; I still wouldn't come near."
Now that was well said. It showed prudence, not fear.
        Taught by experience, only he
        Knew that mistrust of what you see
        Is safety's surest guarantee.

The Ape and the Dolphin

Book IV

I The Lion in Love
To Mlle. de Sévigné

O Sévigné, first of the fair,
Whose charms are a model of grace,
Wholly lovely in manner and face
Except for your cool haughty air,
Would you deign to partake with delight
In a fabulist's innocent game
And hear without shrinking in fright
Of how Love made a lion grow tame?
Love, you must know, has terrible powers
And fortunate truly are those
Who never encounter its blows
Save in stories like this one of ours.
If you dislike the truths that I proffer
It's only the tale that will suffer
For daring with supplicant zeal
At your footstool in homage to kneel.

In the days when beasts knew how to speak
The Lion, like others, aspired
To draw closer to men, rest his cheek
Near some maiden's. That he so desired
Needn't shock you, for back in those days
The traits of beasts earned as much praise
As humans', so great shaggy manes
Could add luster to bravery and brains.

Now it chanced that this lion espied
A fair shepherdess much to his taste
And he went to her father posthaste

And demanded her hand as his bride.
A nice pickle. So fearsome a gent
Was scarcely the mate one would choose
But if it seemed hard to consent
It would be harder still to refuse.
Besides, could he even be sure,
If he dared to declare "There's no hope,"
That the animal's sexy allure
Mightn't lead her one day to elope?
He'd already observed how she'd swoon
At the sight of those long flowing curls.
He could not say directly "The girl's
Not for you." But he could ask a boon.

"Sir," he ventured, "I'm somewhat afraid
Since my daughter's a delicate maid
That when locked in a loving embrace
Your sharp claws might scratch up her face.
Do you mind if I clipped them? And while
I'm about it I could take a file
To your teeth so your kisses can be
Soft and tender, and so more delicious
To you, for her roused ecstasy
Won't be curbed by the fear that they're vicious."

The Lion consented at once
(Love had made him a gullible dunce).
Without teeth, without claws, nude alack,
Like a room that's been totally stripped,
When some dogs were unleashed to attack
He crept away utterly whipped.

Oh, Love, when you fashion your spell
We can bid common prudence farewell.

II The Shepherd and the Sea

In contentment there dwelt by the sea's briny shore
A shepherd whose annual yield from his flock,
     Though not large, was as sure as a rock.
     Moreover, he needed no more.

But at length all the treasures washed up on the beach
Proved so tempting he sold off his whole herd of sheep
And from overseas trading grew haughty and rich
     Till storms buried his wealth fathoms deep.
The poor wretch was reduced to sheep herding again
But no longer as master, just one of the men.
From idyllic dominion he'd tumbled way down
     To the lot of a poor rustic clown.

In time, though, he managed to save up some gold
     And repurchased the sheep that he'd sold.
And, the winds now abated, he saw there might be
A new chance to venture his wealth on the sea.
He scanned its deceptively peaceable swell
And, recalling his earlier fortune's decline,
Growled "Let others lose gold through the lure of your spell.
     I assure you shall not have mine."

Now this isn't a tale just made up to amuse
     For it teaches a truth you can use.
     A few pennies held safe and secure
     Have more value because they are sure
     Than a fortune you're likely to lose.

     Contentment's such a worthy prize
     It's worth our while to shut our eyes
     To the ocean's deceitful allure.
For each one who succeeds, ten thousand fail.
     The glittering promise turns to lies
     When windstorms and pirates prevail.

III The Fly and the Ant

The fly and the ant were debating their worth.
  The former professed to be stunned
That a miserable creature confined to the earth
  Should let self-love so dazzle her mind
As to make her believe that her claims could compare
  With those of the daughter of air.

"Why, I buzz about palaces, feast with the gods,
Even sample the sacrifice placed at their knees
Before they receive it. Now what are the odds
  That your honors are equal to these?
As for feasting, you're lucky if you can get by
On some poor dried-up breadcrumb you've dragged to your lair.
As for lodgings, have you ever perched on the hair
Of an Emperor, a King, or a Beauty? Well, I
Do so often. I've even been known to repair
To more intimate spots where the mark that I place
On a maiden's fair features makes even more fair
The pearly complexion of bosom or face.
No wonder therefore that the finishing touch
Applied in her boudoir's a neat man-made 'mouche.'
  So please spare me your stories, I pray,
  Of the riches you've salted away."

  "Are you finished?" responded the ant.
  "Well, your boasts don't impress me one whit.
  You're accursed in those palaces you haunt
  And the fact that you nibble a bit
Of the food of the gods just before others do
Doesn't lend any special distinction to you.
If you're seen everywhere, well then, so too are mobs.
Now you light on a king's head, and now on some slob's.
Either way such behavior as likely as not
Will promptly result in a death-dealing swat.
  And that business about beauty patches
  Leaves the contest between us a match as

92

I'm equally black. But so what?
You can call those things 'mouches,' for that title of flies
Is given as well to lickspittles and spies.
       The former are chased out of court.
       The latter are hanged. So in short
Drop your haughty professions and own up straightway
That your frail constitution has made you a prey
To hunger and cold and a miserable death
When you're no longer warmed by the West Wind's soft breath.

"Meanwhile I enjoy through the long winter nights
The fruit of my labors, abundant delights
That spare me the need to go trudge through the snow,
The wind and the rain. I sit snugly below
And feast on my food hoard, serenely aware
That my earlier carefulness frees me from care.
       That should prove that the difference between
       True and false claims is easily seen.
But I can't waste my time any more on this matter.
I have work to get done. To replenish my grain
       Calls for diligence, not idle chatter."

IV The Gardener and His Lordship

A gardening enthusiast,
A townsman who held property
In rural precincts, thought that he
Might take an outlying field and close it fast
To make a kitchen garden that would bear
All the quick-growing herbs that flourished there:
Sorrel and lettuce, jessamine and thyme
(To name a few which chance to fit my rhyme).

But his fancy no sooner was turned into fact
Than the tempting fresh greens that grew up in his tract
Were nibbled to bits by a ravenous hare
And he turned to the lord of the land in despair.
"That damn beast is insatiable. Morning and night
He chomps in my garden and nothing I do,
Neither sticks, stones, nor snares can take care of my plight.
I believe he's a sorcerer."
                              "Don't take that view,"
Said his lordship. "I'm sure he's an ordinary hare.
But were he the devil himself, I declare
That in spite of his tricks I could trap him straightway.
Would you like me to get him?"
                              "Yes, just tell me when."
"Why, tomorrow if you wish. There's no need to delay."

And, true to his word, he arrived the next day
At daybreak along with a few dozen men.
"Let's have breakfast first. Tell me, how good are your birds?
And here is your daughter. Now what do you think?
Shall we make her our bride?" he proposed with a wink.
"If we do, understand that your coffers must shrink."
And such bold, brazen actions then followed these words:
Pulling her towards him and stroking her arm,
Lifting her neckerchief—gestures all parried
So adroitly the poor father thought with alarm
That his daughter was setting her cap to be married.

94

Meanwhile the company charged at the table,
Every compliment meant to elicit more food:
"Won't you bring on those hams. They look awfully good."
"Milord, help yourself," said the townsman, unable
To offer resistance. "Delighted, I'm sure"
Was the instant response of the sanguine Seigneur.
So he and his troop, dogs and horses and all,
Made themselves quite at home. It was "Liberty Hall."
They downed their host's wine just as if it was water
While his lordship continued caressing the daughter.

When breakfast was over, more bustling about
Commenced as the huntsmen bestirred to prepare
For the chase to the sound of the trumpet's shrill blare.
And the noise and confusion so frazzled him out
That the townsman was practically tearing his hair.
Even worse was the way that they trampled upon
The poor kitchen garden, destroying in one swoop
The vegetable beds that he'd carefully sown
With chicory and onions to flavor his soup.

In the meantime their quarry, the hare, hunkered down
Beneath a large cabbage. The hunters gave chase.
It escaped through a hole, one not nearly so big
As the one that they made in their clattering race
Through the hedgerows, his lordship not caring a fig.
His horsemen, of course, must be given free rein
And the townsman might shrug but he dared not complain.
In sum, though the culprit was finally caught,
In one single hour more damage was wrought
Than all of the hares in the province could do
Over the course of a century or two.

Petty princes, you're better off settling things
Amongst yourselves rather than calling on kings.
You'd be crazy to make them your allies in war.
            Don't let even one through the door.

V The Donkey and the Little Dog

We should not try unnatural tricks.
We can never perform them with grace.
A bumpkin who hails from the sticks
Cannot take a gentleman's place.
Few and fortunate are those for whom Heaven decrees
At birth both the will and the talent to please.
For the rest, let them take on no more than they're able to
Lest they resemble the ass in the fable who
Rushed to bestow on his master a hug
In the hope he'd be met like a favored lapdog.

He asked himself "Why should it be
Just because that dog's dainty and small
That he's treated affectionately
While I get no caresses at all?
Just see how he's petted and kissed on the nose
While I'm only the object of blows.
What's his secret? He puts out his paw
And at once he is kissed and embraced.
Why, if that's all it takes," he said, setting his jaw,
"It's not that hard to suit Milord's taste."

Whereon, seeing his master, he joyfully clomped to his side
And lifted a battered trombone
To draw forth such sounds as he fondly believed would provide
A flourish to grace the embrace he'd be getting anon.
What a hug he delivered! What a piercingly shrill squealing tone!
Big mistake. All he gets is a vehement cry of dismay.
"Quick, someone, a stick. Drive this horrible creature away."
And the comedy's done.

VI The War Between the Rats and the Weasels

The nation of Weasels,
Like the nation of Cats,
Felt nothing but loathing
For the nation of Rats,
And had rat holes not been
Far too narrow and tight
To let larger beasts in
I imagine they might
Have wiped out those small pests
Now lodged safe in their nests.

But it chanced that one year
The rats' numbers so swelled
That, abandoning fear,
Their hosts took to the field
Led by King Ratapon,
Which they'd no sooner done
Than the weasels advanced
With their banners unfurled
And the battle commenced.
Swords were thrust, lances hurled.

For a long time the tide
Of the battle so swayed
That in turn either side
Thought its fortunes were made
While the fields soaked up blood.
But, at last, like a flood
Sweeping over a plain,
Hordes of weasels dashed out.
All resistance was vain;
Vain the brave last-ditch stand
Of a few of their band.
The rats fled in a rout.
All their generals slain,
Flight their only recourse,

Troops and officers all
Rushed about in full force
Seeking only to crawl
Through some hole in the wall.

For the men quickly done,
For their leaders not so
Since the gear they had on
Was intended to show
Both their rank and their might,
Plumes and helmets with horns
That were meant to affright.
But whatever adorns
Has its negative side
So that when those lords tried
To effect their escape
The extravagant size
And the outlandish shape
Of their martial chapeaux
Left them nowhere to go.
As you well may surmise
They were caught in a vise.
Not a hole, chink or slit
Was sufficiently wide
For such trappings to fit,
So their owners all died.

Fine feathers, alas,
Are mixed blessings at best.
Humble folk often pass
Through life's trials without harm.
Those more splendidly dressed
Have more cause for alarm.

VII The Ape and the Dolphin

'Twas the custom of Greeks long ago
When they took to the sea in their ships
For travelers to carry in tow
Their pets—dancing dogs and young apes.
Now by chance one such ship struck a reef
Still in sight of the port. And I fear
Those on board might have all come to grief
Had not dolphins been swimming quite near.
For as Pliny has sagely opined
(And who dares doubt so learned a man?)
These beasts are good friends of mankind
And will save folk whenever they can.

In this case, mistaking its shape
For a human's, one dolphin espied
And proceeded to rescue an ape
By offering to give it a ride
With such gravity one might have thought
He'd Arion himself on his back,
That famed singer who once had been brought
Safely home from another shipwreck.

Once sure that his guest wouldn't drown,
The dolphin, to make conversation,
Asked "Is Athens, that glorious town,
Your dwelling?"
                              "Oh yes, and my station
Is one of the highest renown,"
The ape boasted. "My dad's occupation
As a judge, and my cousin's at court
Allow me to pledge that they'd serve
To speed your affairs—any sort,
A reward that you richly deserve."

"Many thanks," said the dolphin. "Pray tell,
Is Piraeus a part of your scene?"

"Yes indeed. He's a chap I know well.
I can't tell you how long it has been
That we've met to have lunch every day,"
Said the ape with a fatuous grin,
A remarkably dumb thing to say
—Assuming the port was a man.

There are people who act the same way,
Prattling on, self-assured, unaware
It's their ignorance that's on display
As they boast "I know that. I've been there."
They go on about Paris and Rome
And their many connections abroad
When the fact is they've never left home.
No surprise folks are on to their fraud.

Just so, at his passenger's raving
The dolphin looked back and perceived
What a babbling baboon he was saving.
"Who needs this?" he declared, undeceived.
And, shrugging the wretch off his back,
He dove down, just as you might expect
To put himself onto the track
Of a human who'd earn his respect.

VIII The Man and the Wooden Idol

A pagan once worshipped an idol of wood,
A god who was deaf though he'd ears on his head,
But the pagan was sure that, when pleased, this god could
Not just hear but respond to the prayers that he said.
So he poured out his wealth in an unending flow
Of offerings—whole oxen with garlands adorned.
There was never an idol who profited so
Yet all the poor worshiper's wishes were scorned—
No inheritance, no treasure, not even the gain
From a good hand at cards. His devotion was vain.
Still he didn't give up. The least prospect of harm
Called for a gift, and the idol amassed
More wealth while the man lost all—cash, home and farm,
         And his anger exploded at last.

He took up a crowbar and smashed into bits
The cause of his downfall—and what did he see
But a whole heap of gold. "Was I out of my wits?
When I fed you so well, you gave nothing to me.
You phony, clear out; find some other poor dupe.
I finally see through your rascally tricks.
With a monster like you the one way to recoup
My lost treasure," he said, "is with bludgeons and sticks.
         I starved so you could lie in clover.
                 Thank God, my folly's over."

101

IX The Jay Dressed Up in Peacock Feathers

A peacock having molted, a jay came along
       And fastened its plumes to his own.
So bedecked, he then proudly paraded among
       Other peacocks, convinced that he shone.
Of course he fooled no one. They jeered and they mocked
And sniggered "This visitor's strangely befrocked."
But when he sought refuge among his own kind
He fared no whit better. They showed him the door.
No surprise. For his impudent airs bring to mind
       Other popinjays equally blind
Who flaunt borrowed finery fashioned before
By their betters. I mean plagiarists, not to mince words.
But enough. Why be bothered to say any more
       About such contemptible birds?

X The Camel and the Floating Sticks

The first time a camel was spied
Those who saw it ran off terrified.
The next time they approached. Then at last one man dared
To harness the brute. They no longer were scared.
So familiarization in time serves to change
Our view of what once had seemed awesome and strange.

This calls to mind another tale
Of watchmen staring out to sea
Who spied far off what seemed a sail
And told themselves it had to be
A mighty vessel on the main.
But as it neared they looked again
Perceiving that they must revise
Their judgment of its shape and size.
"It's just a skiff."
                    "No, it's a raft."
Their final verdict, as the "craft"
Drew closer: "Just some floating sticks."

How often it is that the mind's eye plays tricks.
Distant objects that scare us half out of our skin
Turn out to be nothing as they get closer in.

XI The Frog and the Rat

How often, notes Merlin, one's plans to ensnare
        Another rebound on their source.
Though folks mock this wise saw as old-hat, I declare
        That its lesson still carries great force.

Let me illustrate, citing the tale of a rat,
        Nicely rounded, enticingly plump
(He'd never let fast days diminish his fat),
        Who was strolling one day near a swamp
When up popped a frog who addressed him straightway
        With an offer he couldn't refuse.
"Won't you come to my house for a banquet today?"
        "Yes indeed."
                "Then prepare for a cruise.
We must sail through these waters to get there," said she,
        "But the pleasures en route are so rare
That years hence you'll recount all the marvels you see
        To your grandchildren, making them stare.
You'll see all the buildings, the customs and rites
        Of the folk who inhabit this bog
And you'll never behold such incomparable sights
        Though you roam the world," promised the frog.

Her lavish descriptions were lost on the rat
        But the prospect of food made him game.
He jumped into the bog but at once realized that
        As a swimmer he was at best lame.
"Don't despair," said the frog. "Here's a nice piece of twine
        That I plucked from a reed near the shore.
I can fasten your foreleg securely to mine
        And you needn't be scared anymore."
But, once in the water, the traitor dived down,
        Her motive now shockingly clear.
"What a delicate morsel you'll make when I drown
        You, Sir Rat," she announced with a sneer.

He appealed to the gods, but she laughed in his face.
        He struggled; she tugged. As they fought,
A kite who was circling over that place
        Saw a chance that he'd not even sought.

                Two for one. Down he swooped
                From his home in the skies.
                One deft turn and he scooped
                Up his unforeseen prize.
                "Flesh and fish both tonight.
                What a treat!" said the kite.

                The most well-crafted plot
                Oftentimes comes to naught
                And as likely as not
                It's the plotter who's caught.

XII The Animals' Tribute to Alexander

Here's a fable once current in ages gone by
But its moral escapes me somehow.
Perhaps you may see it more quickly than I
So I'll just tell the bare story now.

Through Fame's trumpet a message was sent far and wide
That a certain Alexander of half-divine birth
Demanded the homage befitting his pride
And required every creature on earth:
Quadrupeds, humans, huge beasts, tiny worms,
All the birds of the air right away
To forswear henceforth freedom's long-cherished charms
And submit on bent knee to his sway.

Alarmed by the many-tongued goddess's call,
The animals, thoroughly cowed,
Felt this Emperor's stern edict must hold them in thrall;
They would only be spared if they bowed.
So, quitting their lairs, they assembled en masse,
Debating, resolving all night
Till they drew up a measure that managed to pass:
To appease their new lord's appetite
They would send a legation prepared to bow low
In homage and also to offer
The tribute accorded a conquering foe
If they only could fill a rich coffer.
With the ape put in charge, someone thought of a plan
To handle that need. They'd apply
To a prince who had gold mines within his domain
And would give them a generous supply.
That settled, the next task was how to convey
This treasure. No obstacle there.
Mule, donkey and horse, camel too rushed to say
That they'd willingly carry their share.
So they went on their way till they happened to meet

106

Seigneur Lion. (They weren't at all pleased.)
"Oh, how timely," he smirked. "Now your group is complete.
Any fears you may have will be eased.
And you'll help me out too. I'd originally planned
To bring a small gift of my own.
But it looks too pathetic. If it could be joined
With yours, why the total has grown.
All will benefit thus. For with me as your guard
Should we meet any thieves, you'll be spared.
But I can't be encumbered. You'll not find it hard,
I trust, if my portion is shared.
With each of you taking one fourth on your back,
My powerful limbs will be free
To destroy any villain who dares to attack."
What choice had they except to agree?

The arrangement was made. Once relieved of his load
The lion was pleased to partake
Of the liberal provisions supplied for the road
With no thought of who'd put up the stake.
They wandered along till they came to a spot
Amply watered, refreshingly cool,
Whereupon Seigneur Lion declared he felt hot
And must plunge for relief in a pool.
"I've a fever," he gasped. "You must leave me behind
And continue your journey alone.
But before you depart would you please be so kind
As to give me back what is my own."

What to do? They unpacked, and the lion cried out
In a tone of unmeasured delight,
"Just see what a splendid result's come about.
My coins have borne babes overnight.
And what's even more thrilling, the babies have grown
Till they equal their mothers in size.
So I'll take back my portion." As soon said as done.
For his hosts, horror vied with surprise.

107

They dared not protest though the meager amount
He left them was clearly unfair
As they duly complained when they gave their account
On presenting that pitiful share
To the great Alexander. And what did he do?
Simply laugh at their helpless chagrin.
In a contest of lions, his majesty knew,
Humbler beings had best not mix in.

XIII The Horse Who Sought
Vengeance Against the Stag

Horses weren't put on earth for the sake of mankind,
And when humans still lived in a primitive state
With acorns the principal food that they ate
Any equine at all wasn't easy to find.
How unlike our own day when you'd have to be blind
Not to catch sight of them early and late.

> Saddled, harnessed, loaded down,
> Pulling wagons into town,
> Clad in armor, off to war,
> What service aren't they drafted for
> Since their life's become refined?

How did it start? There was a horse
Who'd had a run-in with a stag
And tried to chase him down. Of course
He was out of his league. He began to flag.
Winded and desperate, he had recourse
To a human being whose sharper wit
Might serve his cause. It did. The man
Fitted his mouth with a racing bit
And leaped on his back and away they ran,
Not stopping at all to catch their breath
Till the stag was caught and put to death.

"Many thanks," said the horse. "I am in your debt.
Now farewell. I am off to my home in the woods."
"What's the rush?" said the man. "Don't leave just yet.
Why not stay and partake of my plentiful goods?
You'll be treated well, I guarantee,
If you consent to dwell with me."
Done—at a cost he could not foresee,
The forfeiture of his liberty.

The horse realized his folly when it was too late,
Trapped behind his stable door,

Barred from passing beyond its gate,
Doomed to servitude forevermore.
How much wiser to have shrugged off the stag's offense.
The joy of revenge is too dearly bought
If it comes at the purchaser's expense,
Losing freedom, that gift without which all is naught.

XIV The Fox and the Sculptured Bust

Men of title are mostly all surface and show
Whose fine features conceal what is hidden below.
Vulgar fools only judge by the masks that they see
But, unlike those poor asses, the fox probes and pries
To the depths from all angles, his acuity
       Cutting down their pretensions to size.

"They remind me, I fear, of a grand sculpted head
       Of a hero I've often espied.
It was larger than life, but the sculptor," he said,
       "Left it perfectly hollow inside.
Such a beautiful head, but without any brains."
To how many of our Lordships that saying pertains.

XV The Wolf, the Nanny Goat and the Kid
XVI The Wolf, the Mother and the Child

Needing nourishment herself, a mother goat
       Had to leave her kid behind
       As she ventured out to find
       Pasturage not too remote
       While it stayed at home to wait.
       But before she left her den
       With great care she locked the gate.
       "Don't let anybody in,"
       She warned, "precious child of mine,
       Who does not know how to say
       These few words, our special sign,
       'Let all wolves keep far away.'"

       But a wolf just chanced to pass
       As she spoke and overheard
       By coincidence, alas,
       And remembered every word.
       The poor mother hadn't seen
       Her old nemesis at all,
       So no sooner was she gone
       Than he paid the kid a call
And, speaking in a bland and sugared tone,
He mouthed the password "Wolves keep far away"
And asked to be let in immediately.
"Not quite so fast," he heard to his dismay.
"Before I do there's something I must see."

Rightly suspicious that the words alone
Guaranteed nothing, the kid refused to budge.
Just opening the sill a tiny crack,
"Show your white paws," he said, "that I may judge
Whether I'm safe from a surprise attack."
White paws, of course, are almost never found
On wolves. The kid's request had foiled his plan.

Surprised and outmaneuvered, the villain frowned
And slunk back, disappointed, to his den.

    As this episode makes clear
    When one's life's in jeopardy
    One cannot be cavalier.
    Double's proof's no luxury.

  This wolf recalls another tale
  Of a fellow wolf, which I'll relate.
  He also sought an easy meal
  But suffered a more grievous fate.
He too observed a parent leave his home,
A villager who often in the past
Brought back with him a wide array of game:
Turkeys and sheep and calves. No need to fast
When the man returned. But oh, the wait seemed slow.
He'd almost figured it was time to go
    When from just inside the cot
    He made out an infant's cry
    Which at once was followed by
    A sharp warning to the tot:
"Be still or I will call the wolf right now
To eat you up." The baby just cried harder.
"The gods be praised," Wolf voiced a pious vow,
"For sending me this providential larder."

But as he approached, he was startled to hear
A different message, "Stop crying, my pet.
I promise there's no need to worry or fret.
We'll kill that bad wolf if he dares to appear."
"What's this?" cried the wolf. "See how quickly they change
Their tune. Do they think I'm an absolute fool?
And how will they feel when this child dares to range
Through the woods years from now on his way home from school?"

Just then, from all sides angry peasants stormed out
With pitchforks and dogs and all manner of gear.
"Explain yourself. What are you looking for here?"

The wolf told his tale, for he hadn't a doubt
That the mother's own words would put him in the clear.
"What! You think I would want you to gobble my child?
How can you give such falsehoods breath?"
The crowd agreed, and going wild,
They beat the wretched wolf to death.
They cut off his head and his right foot as well
And carried them off to the local seigneur,
Who mounted them both on a placard that bore
A warning to wolves wheresoever they dwell:
"Gentlemen, never be taken in by
Scolding words used by mothers to children who cry."

XVII What Socrates Said

When Socrates first built his home
Scarcely a soul approved the plan.
"Far too plain," said one critic. "It should have a dome."
        "It isn't worthy of the man,"
Another complained. And everyone agreed
That the quarters were smaller than what he'd need.
        "Why there's hardly room to turn around.
That's not where such eminence should be found."

"Thank heaven for a few true friends," said he.
"For them its dimensions will do just fine."
        How very right he was to see
That the rest had no place in his design.
"I am your friend," it's so easy to declare.
The word *friend* is as common as a word can be.
        But the thing itself is far more rare.

XVIII The Old Man and His Children

Power can't be sustained once its parts are dispersed.
That's a sober fact Aesop displayed to us first.
You must understand, though, that I rewrite his story
Just to make it more current, not challenge his glory.
It was Phaedrus who consciously aimed to excel
His model—and often succeeded, but to tell
My version to better my betters would be
Too vain an ambition. That said, let's agree
To move on and observe how a father's desire
To enlighten his sons could so badly misfire.

An old man at death's door called his sons to his bed.
"I have something to show you, dear children," he said.
"Here's a bundle of sticks. Try to break them in two.
I'll explain what this teaches you after you do."
So the eldest tried first. How he struggled and strained.
"This takes someone much stronger than me," he complained.
The next took his turn and had no more success.
Then the youngest attacked but soon had to confess
That he too was no match for that tightly bound sheaf.
"Now," the father declared, "since you've all come to grief,
Let me demonstrate just how these poor feeble hands
Can do what you couldn't and break up these wands."

They thought he was joking. He proved they were wrong.
He untied the bundle. No stick was so strong
That he couldn't just snap it without any strain.
"There's a moral in this, boys, I now can make plain.
If you all stick together you can't be defeated."
Having passed on this wisdom, his life's work completed,
He faced with composure the prospect of death,
Only asking his sons with his last dying breath
To promise they'd always be there for each other
United in all affairs, brother to brother.

In tears, all three promised. He died with a smile.
But he'd only been dead for a very short while
When the brothers discovered he'd left his affairs
In a horrible mess. Who could tell what was theirs?
With creditors hounding and lawsuits galore
They tried to be true to the oath that they swore.
And they were—a whole week. Then you know what came next.
They differed on how to interpret a text.
Ties of blood and sworn oaths were no match for the power
Of greedy self-interest aroused from that hour.
They bickered and quibbled and took their dispute
To a judge who found fault with all three in their suit.
His opinion spurred others to come forth anew
And opened a floodgate of further suits too.
And they couldn't agree any better when faced
With outside opposition. If one had a taste
For compromise, two would insist they hold fast.
Well, you won't be surprised by what happened at last.
Through all of their wrangling they lost their estate.
If a lesson was learned, it was learned much too late.

XIX The Oracle and the Infidel

The hope of deceiving the powers above
Is a folly mankind is too capable of,
Unaware that our species' most crooked designs
Are as clear to the gods as the clearest of signs,
And the darkness we use to escape from their gaze
          Is pierced through by their all-seeing rays.

A pagan whose views on such matters as these
Had a skeptical edge once decided to tease
Apollo himself, since by chance or design
          He had come to that deity's shrine.

"Tell me, great God Apollo," he boldly began,
"What I hold in my hand, is it living or dead?"
What he held was a sparrow. His devious plan
Was to prove the reverse of whatever was said
          By strangling or sparing. But his game
Was a farce to Apollo, who saw through his scheme.
"Just show me that sparrow and stop playing tricks
Or you'll find your own self in a life-or-death fix.
As I see from afar, try what nonsense you like,
          Just as well from afar I can strike."

XX The Miser Who Lost His Treasure

Till we put it to use nothing really is ours.
I challenge those folk who devote all their powers
To heaping up wealth that they never dare touch
To prove others are poorer who don't hoard as much.
The miser who chooses to live like a wretch
In life as in death is exactly as rich
As Diogenes, the cynic who dwelt in a ditch.

This truth can be seen in the tale Aesop told
       Of the rich man who buried his gold.
This unfortunate chap was so weak in the head
As to think it would follow him when he was dead
To finally purchase deferred happiness.
Postponing all pleasure, he didn't possess
       His wealth; it possessed him instead.
Not only his gold but his soul could be found
       Cached away in a hole in the ground,
The thought of its splendor his only delight
       Consuming him morning and night.

Whether coming or going, eating or drinking,
Our miser was occupied only in thinking
Of the spot where his treasure had been laid away,
A spot that he frequented day after day,
So often a gravedigger shrewdly suspected
It held something of value that might be collected,
And when no one was looking he dug up the loot.
The miser returned, saw the hole and, struck mute
At first by the shock, soon was tearing his hair
And sobbing and groaning in utter despair.

A passerby drawn to this pitiful sight
Inquired, "Dear sir, what's the cause of your plight?"
"It's my treasure. Some thief has made off with it all."
"Why, where did he find it?"
"Buried right near that wall."

119

"But how come it was there? Since we aren't at war
What possibly could you be hiding it for?
Why not keep it at home so it's there on the shelf
When you want to buy something you'd like for yourself?"
"Buy something? My God!" He was really perturbed.
"Don't you know that this treasure must not be disturbed?"

"So you didn't mean to spend it? Why then so much grief?
You haven't been actually harmed by that thief.
Put a stone in its place and then surely enough,
For all that it matters, you'll be no worse off."

XXI The Master's Eye

A stag seeking refuge ducked into a stable.
        He was warned by the oxen to flee.
        "It's not really safe here, you'll see,"
They chided. But he, using sweet talk, was able
To get them to promise they wouldn't betray
His presence, while he in return would repay
        Their kindness by showing them a lea
Full of grasses and herbs so abundant and sweet
They'd be grateful for many a year for the treat.
So he hid in a corner and got back his breath.
(From running so hard he'd been brought near to death.)

Sometime later the farmhands came bearing fresh hay
And fodder, the same chore they did every day.
To and fro, in and out, at their master's behest
They went dozens of times while the unbidden guest
Was noticed by no one, not even their chief.
They left and the stag heaved a sigh of relief.
"I can make my escape without further delay."

"Not so fast," said an ox. "One thing stands in your way.
An inspector is coming whose Argus-eyed stare
Can spot something amiss though it's just by a hair.
It's the Master himself. There he is at the door.
With one single glance he can take in far more
Than that whole other lot." And indeed that proved true.
The chastising words of reproof fairly flew:
"These stalls need more grass and that litter's not fresh.
Would it hurt you to carry away all this trash?
Or to sweep off these spiders and straighten this gear?
Is this how you care for my——What have we here?
A head crowned with antlers? Now that's something new."
And the poor stag was finally seen by the crew.
They took up their pikestaffs. Their prey had no chance.
His fate had been sealed by the master's keen glance

(Not to mention the prospect of many a feast
Once they'd properly butchered and salted the beast).

As Phaedrus observed in his elegant way,
No eye sees like a master's when turned to survey
Whatever possessions come under his sway
—Except for a lover's, I'm prompted to say.

XXII The Lark, Her Young Ones, and the Owner of a Field

"Self-reliance"—That motto is preached everywhere.
      Here's a tale Aesop told
        To unfold
How that lesson plays out, using birds of the air.

He pictured a lark at that flush time of year
When the promptings of amorous rebirth
Stir every creature here on earth,
Fish, flesh, and fowl. This aroused pioneer,
Though she'd not found a mate, was determined to rear
A family of her own, and it seemed to her best,
Since the spring was half over, to feather her nest
At once, lay her eggs, and then hatch out her young.
All went well. And the ripening wheat fields among
Which it sheltered provided at least for a while
A hiding place safe for her still unfledged brood,
Allowing the lark to range many a mile
In her anxious adventures in search of fresh food.

Every day when she left them she warned them anew
To be on their guard and to pay special heed
Whenever the owner of the field might come through
To the words he exchanged with his son. "For indeed
Their message will give us a critical clue
To the moment our safety is not guaranteed.
At that point," she declared, "we must instantly flee."

Not long after, the owner observed to his son
"These wheat fields look ripe. Call our friends, every one,
And bid them assemble tomorrow at dawn
To bring in the crops with a full company."
      When the lark returned that night
      She found her offspring wild with fright.
"We heard him say clearly he'd call up his neighbors
To help him at dawn with his harvesting labors."

123

"Don't worry, my chicks. If that's all that he said
We can each sleep securely tonight in our bed.
Eat your dinner, relax, but tomorrow I ask
That you once again take up the very same task
And listen to pick up precisely what words
He uses," admonished that wisest of birds.

The next day proved her right. Not one neighbor arrived.
"Now I can't do a thing," said the man, both aggrieved
And ashamed that he'd let himself be so deceived
As to count on the help of so lazy a crew.
          "Son, here is what you'll have to do.
Run to my parents; repeat my request."
Imagine the terror that now seized the nest.
"This time we are certainly doomed, we're afraid.
He's called on his kinfolk to come to his aid."
          "No, my children, sleep in peace.
          We needn't budge yet from our place."

Again she was right. Again no one appeared.
"That's it," said the farmer. "It's just as I feared.
I was stupid to think I could safely rely
On the good will of others to further my ends.
No parent or friend loves me better than I.
A man's own two arms are his very best friends.
So tomorrow our household will go out alone.
We'll each wield a sickle and get the job done."

When her nestlings reported these words to the lark
          She sighed, "Now there's the fateful clue.
          We must steal away while it's still dark.
          From what you say I know it's true
          That what he plans he'll surely do."

The Satyr and the Traveler

Book V

I Mercury and the Woodcutter
To M.L.C.D.B.

Sir, your taste as a reader's long served as my guide
And I've done what I can so that taste's satisfied.
You dislike polished phrases and overwrought lines
That speak of excessively vaulting designs.
I do too. Yes, an author is likely to spoil
The effect that he seeks through too sedulous toil.
Still there are some nice touches we both would let stay.
You really like them; I think they're okay.
And as for the point Aesop made in each fable,
I tuck it in somehow as well as I'm able,
But if I don't manage to please or to teach
Don't blame me; something always lies just beyond reach.

     With my limited force
     I've no other resource
Than sly mockery staged from behind its butt's back
Instead of a righteous full-frontal attack.
Wit's the one gift I have, and it may not suffice
Assailed as it is by a double-edged vice,
Foolish vanity and envy together in league,
     Our modern age's ruling plague
     Where every puny wretched beast
     Would be a mighty bull at least.

Sometimes I balance both sides of the scale,
Vice and virtue, sense and folly opposed in each tale.
Wolves and lambs, flies and ants play the comedy out
With lessons that may not delight the devout

In hundreds of variants ranging worldwide
　　　　Observing life from every side.
Man, gods, and beasts, every one plays a part.
Even the highest of gods is a prop for my art,
His romantic adventures set forth on display,
Though not in the story I've chosen today.

A woodcutter in days gone by it's said
Had lost the axe with which he earned his bread.
He searched all over but his search was vain.
"I'm done for now," he wept in grief and pain.
It would break your heart to hear the way he groaned.
That was the only useful tool he owned.
"Oh Jupiter, please give it back to me,"
He cried. "Don't leave me to my misery."

Up on Olympus Jupiter heard his cry
And sent an emissary from on high.
Mercury told the woodsman "Don't despair.
It isn't lost, I'm sure. Search everywhere."
He searched. Surprise! He found one made of gold.
"But that's not what I had," the god was told.
A silver axe came next. "That's still no good.
I only want my own axe made of wood."
"Well, you shall have it, and your honesty
Deserves to be rewarded. Take all three."

He did. No sooner had the tale gone round
Than everywhere you turned you'd hear the sound
Of woodsmen wailing "Jupiter, we plead.
Please give us back the axes that we need."
"What's going on here?" asked the king of gods.
"It's time to tell the true claims from the frauds.
Mercury, descend and offer all who cry
The golden axe. Then see how they reply."

He went. Each claimant thought, I'd be a fool
Not to accept at once that golden tool
And say "That's mine. Thank God you've brought it back."
So they got nothing but an angry whack.

Rather than stoop to lying out of greed
Far better to accept just what we need.
It's not just wrong, it's stupid, for no doubt
Whatever you try, the gods will find you out.

II The Earthen Pot and the Iron Pot

The iron pot suggested
A trip to the earthen pot
But the earthen pot resisted
And said he'd rather not.
"I'll be safer," he replied
"Here at my own fireside.
I'm not really very strong
And if I should come along
There's no way I could recover
From any accident whatever.
As for you, you're strong enough.
Your trip needn't be put off."

"But you have no need to fear.
For protection I'll be near,"
Said his sanguine, sturdy friend.
"I'll be with you to the end
And I'll promptly interpose
My tough frame against all blows.
I am certain I can block
The most unexpected shock."

Vows so confident and kind
Caused the pot to change his mind.
No need further to delay,
So they set out on their way
Bumping merrily down the road,
But with every step they strode
On their stubby little feet,
Every hiccup's jarring beat,
They were thrown against each other
And although it didn't bother
The iron pot, the story was quite different for his mate

Who was smashed to bits not many yards beyond the garden gate
          With no time to even groan.
So don't socialize with those whose rank's too different from your own
          Lest you meet the selfsame fate
          As the pot made out of stone.

III The Little Fish and the Fisherman

A little fish in time may grow
If the good Lord allows it to
But the fisherman who lets it go
Commits a folly in my view,
For he's not very likely to catch it again.
Thus, one day when a small fry was caught in a seine
The fisherman cheerfully bagged it and said
"Every little bit counts. I am that much ahead.
By itself it may not make a very fine feast
    But it is a beginning at least."

The poor fish of course took a different line.
"Do you really believe you'll be able to dine
    On such a meager mite as I?
    Why you'd be lucky," said the fry,
    "To get one mouthful. I suggest
    That it would serve your interests best
    To toss me back and land a prize
    When I am grown to adult size.
    By then, believe me, I should weigh
    One hundred times my weight today.
I'll go further. I'll bet that one hundred small fish
Like me wouldn't even make one proper dish.
Let me go and I promise you'll get something nice
To eat—or to sell for a far better price.
    At present I'm worthless."
                    "Indeed?" said the man.
"I can see why you say so. You're hoping you can
With all your fine arguments flee from your fate,
The frying pan first, then the place on my plate.
    Poor fellow, your plea comes too late.
No matter how small, what I've already got
    Is certain. The future is not."

132

IV The Ears of the Hare

When a beast bearing horns chanced to wound with some blows
      King Lion, in wrath he arose
      And issued a royal decree:
      Every creature with horns had to flee.
      They were banished immediately.
Whether stags with wide antlers or she goats or rams,
Even great broad-browed bulls, all must give up their homes,
      Either that or face imminent death.

When a hare saw the shadow his long ears projected,
He gasped with a shuddering breath
Convinced by their contours that he'd be suspected.
      It was only too clear they resembled
      Real horns; he was done for. He trembled.

"Farewell, neighbor cricket," he called as he fled.
"I've no doubt that they'll say I have horns on my head."
"They're just ears," said the cricket. "Your statement's absurd.
You might as well say that a cricket's a bird."

"But when zealots are roused, simple truth can't prevail.
Were I even to trim them, it wouldn't avail.
However I argue and protest and plead,
   The powers that be will pay no heed.
   "Of course they're horns," they'll say. "We need
   To lock this fellow up. How sad!
      He's gone completely mad."

V The Fox Who Lost His Tail

A fox who'd flourished in his day
As a cruncher of chickens and hunter of hares,
    Who'd scented danger miles away,
    Grown old, was taken unawares
    And found himself a trapper's prey.

By dint of much squirming he made his escape
But he didn't have the luck to be let off scot free.
His tail was the payment he left in the trap.
Being wily, however, he reasoned "Maybe,"
As he skulked away, burning with shame,
"I can sweet talk some others to take up the same
Appearance." And so (his rear still in a bandage)
At the foxes' next council he got up and said
"Why should we be vexed with a useless appendage
That only gets draggled and trailed in the mud?
Just cut it off, fellows." His audience frowned.

Then one of them said, with an undisguised wink,
"What you say sounds appealing but just turn around
And you'll hear for yourself what these 'fellows' all think."
Which he did and immediately heard his words drowned
By catcalls and hooting. So his stratagem fails
And to this day all foxes have tails.

VI The Old Woman and Her Two Servants

There was an old woman whose household employed
Two maids so hard-working their mistress enjoyed
The fruit of their labors with never a care.
And their industry was just the least of their traits
For they spun cloth so fine that you couldn't compare
Even the stuff of the fabulous Fates.
Moreover, they knew all their duties so well
That they needed no watching. But sorry to tell,
They were driven so hard that from earliest light
They were kept at their tasks till well into the night,
Spinning and weaving without any rest.
Then at cockcrow their mistress descended half-dressed
Into their bedroom, a lamp in her hand,
To wake them and work them both at her command.

How hard they resisted. Eyes half-closed, neither stirred
And they gritted their teeth. "Oh, that miserable bird,"
They muttered. "It's his fault we can't even lie
In our beds in the morning. That rooster must die."
In no time at all the thought led to the deed.
They throttled the rooster and cut off his head.
Alas! They were no better off, for instead
Of the rooster, the villain now shaking their bed
Was their mistress, who grudged them the least idle hour
And who shrieked like a ghoul to establish her power.

So often it is when we hope to amend
        A sorry lot, we learn the bitter truth.
Things may not come about the way we planned.
We escape Charybdis' rock to plunge in the end
        Into dread Scylla's mouth.

VII The Satyr and the Traveler

Deep in a lair in the woods
A shaggy satyr dwelt.
He had no worldly goods.
His food was mast and spelt.

With his wife and many a child
He settled snug and tight.
Who needs luxuries in the wild?
Enough to have appetite.

Once when the rain pelted down
There arrived at his rustic den
A traveler chilled to the bone.
The satyr invited him in

And brought him a steaming brew
But before accepting the cup
The guest lifted his hands and blew
To warm his fingers up.

Then, holding the dish in his hand,
The traveler blew gently once more.
Said the satyr "I don't understand.
What are you doing that for?"

"This breath was to cool down my soup.
The first was to get my hands warm."
Said the satyr "You'll have to get up
And go out again into the storm."

"The gods would be angry, I swear
If I sheltered a creature so bold
That with the self-same mouth he'd dare
To blow both hot and cold."

VIII The Horse and the Wolf

In early spring when the gentle airs
Blown from the West revive the earth
And beasts come forth from their winter lairs
To savor the first of the fields' rebirth,
A wolf grown lean through harsh winter's days
Spotted a horse set out to graze.
There's no need to describe his delight
As he took in that promising sight.

"You're no sheep to be sure, but you might as well be
Though to prove it may call for some acting by me.
Well, why not? And I know quite precisely the part
      To play to succeed in my ruse.
I'll declare I'm well versed in the medical art
      And can show him what simples to use
To cure any ailment. Moreover, if he
      Will trust me and name his disease
(For the fact that his master has let him run free
Attests to the presence of some malady)
      I won't even charge any fees."
Approaching the horse, he delivered his spiel
      And got a prompt reply:
      "I've got a strange lump in my heel."
      "My child, you're in luck I passed by.
I'm a specialist in horse care, and I see that you've got
      Trouble in a most tricky spot
      And surgery might be required."
      What a chance to do as he desired,
To leap on his prey who had claimed to be sick.
But the horse was no fool and delivered a kick
      So forcefully it turned to jelly
      His teeth and jaws and underbelly.

137

"Well, that ought to teach me," he ruefully swore.
        "Stick to your last' is wisely said.
        Playing the doctor was dumb for sure
        When slaughter is my proper trade."

IX The Laborer and His Children

Work hard; be diligent.
There's no surer way to thrive.
At death's door a wealthy farmer sent
For his sons to warn while he still was alive
Against selling away the inheritance passed down
By his father before him. Said he
"There's a treasure on this property.
I don't know where exactly, but one thing's well known:
Persistence pays off. You must find it at last
If you dig up our acres once harvest time's past
With shovels and spades. Don't skip one single field
And you'll see what a profit they yield."

Once their father was dead the sons promptly set out
To act on his advice. How they scurried about.
They dug a whole year and they never found gold
But their crop yield increased twentyfold.

What a wise man he was to reveal by this measure
That hard work in itself is a treasure.

X The Mountain Who Gave Birth

A mountain wracked by labor
Pains let out so fierce a wail
She persuaded every neighbor
She'd delivered without fail
A great city encompassing many a house.
Her offspring was a mouse.

When I recollect this fable
Whose facts we may well doubt
But whose meaning we are able
To construe, I think about
Those authors who boast "I will trumpet the story
Of the gods' feats of war in their terror and glory."
They promise great things but produce in the end
Only wind.

XI Luck and the Schoolboy

On the edge of a pit fathoms deep
A schoolboy lay stretched out asleep.
Young boys, you know, sleep without care
On the ground, on the road, anywhere.
Any sensible man in his place
Would have backed off to leave a safe space.

But, happily, Luck reached his side
And gently awakened the lad
Saying "Little one, if you had died
Everybody would say 'Oh, how sad.
His luck ran out.' But I'm not to blame.
Acknowledge your folly in shame
And resolve to be wiser next time.
It's your acts, not my whims, that most often hold sway."
And so saying, she went on her way.

I happen to think that she's right.
Anywhere, anytime, day or night,
We're too apt to ignore circumstance
And credit all outcomes to chance.
Are we foolish or careless or sloppy at work?
Admitting our faults is a task we all shirk.
Whenever we flounder we sing the same song:
It's just our bad luck things go wrong.

XII The Doctors

Doctor Gloomy attended a patient whose care
Was not his alone; Doctor Hopeful was there
And thought he could cure him. His colleague thought not.
"Let him settle his debts in the short time he's got
For he'll soon meet his maker." The sick man, confused
By such differing claims, in the end just refused
Further treatment. "Let Nature decide this," he said
And very soon after, the poor man was dead.

"I was right," Dr. Gloomy triumphantly cried.
"When an outcome's ordained, there's no reason to strive
To reverse it." "You're wrong," Dr. Hopeful replied.
"If he'd listened to me, he would still be alive."

XIII The Hen that Laid the Golden Eggs

Insatiable greed that can never say "Whoa!
I'm well-off enough now" finds its whole fortune go
As we see in the tale of that marvelous hen
Who laid a gold egg for her master each day.
Not content, he determined to kill her and then
Cut her up to retrieve the great treasure that lay,
He believed, in her innards. But to his surprise
There was nothing within. He had ruined his prize.

You latter-day graspers consumed by the itch
For instant rewards, keep this lesson in sight.
The rash moves that you make in your lust to grow rich
   Will make you grow poor overnight.

XIV The Donkey Carrying Relics

A donkey who bore as his load
Holy relics was pleased to believe
Men adored him. He visibly glowed
Sure that incense, those hymns were all his to receive.

Someone chose to correct him and said
"Foolish fellow, just open your eyes.
It's not you to whom men bow their head.
On your back is what they idolize."

Such delusions, I'm sorry to tell,
Aren't indulged in by asses alone.
Though a judge is a fool people still
Will continue to worship his gown.

XV The Stag and the Vine

A stag chased by hunters found refuge at last
In the lee of a large and luxuriant vine,
So well hidden therein his pursuers rode past.
Though the hounds kept on baying, they shrugged off that sign
And called them away. The stag, now feeling safe
Ungratefully started to browse on the leaf
That had saved him. The noise made the hunters turn back
      And succeed in a fatal attack.

"It's what I deserve. Ingrates, learn from my case,"
Were the stag's final words as he fell in the place
That had once been his shelter. "How can I complain
Or sue others for mercy when I chose not to see
The debt that I owed, but went on to profane
      The asylum provided for me."

XVI The Serpent and the File

Have you heard of the snake who felt hungry and crept
To the shop of a watchmaker living nearby
In search of his dinner but found nothing that leapt
       As a prospect in front of his eye
Except a steel file. He proceeded to gnaw
At its edge. The file gently expounded the flaw
In his thinking. "Poor simpleton, can you not see
       You've more than met your match in me?
       Attack me and you'll find, you clown,
       It's I who grind away, not you.
       All of your teeth will be filed down
       Before you've gotten a grain or two."

Think of that lesson, you second-rate hacks
Who, having no merits, make up for your lacks
       By "biting" whatever's in sight.
True beauty and worth, strong as fire-forged steel,
Will thwart your weak efforts and teach you to feel
       How vain's your debased appetite.

XVII The Hare and the Partridge

We must never mock those more unhappy than we
For we cannot be sure our own luck will hold out.
      As Aesop shows us, frequently
      Fate takes a sudden turnabout.
      There are many examples that I could name
      But the moral is always the same.

Consider the case of a neighborly pair,
Miss Partridge and, in the same meadow, young Hare.
Their lives seemed quite tranquil until suddenly
The approach of a large pack of hounds made him flee.
He rushed to his lair and was soon out of sight,
      His pursuers baffled one and all,
Till one caught the scent that the heat of his flight
Had wafted abroad. The poor creature's downfall
Was only a matter of minutes. He died
Trapped in that spot that he'd chosen to hide.

The heartless partridge jeered, "You thought
You were so swift you couldn't get caught.
So much for your prowess." But even as she spoke
The laugh was on her. It was her turn to die.
She'd trusted her wings to uplift her so high
That she'd be out of reach. But a low-flying hawk
Saw her and swooped. In an instant his claws
      Delivered his prey to his jaws.

XVIII The Eagle and the Owl

The owl and the eagle decided one day
To end their old quarrels, just put them away.
They embraced and they swore solemn oaths. From now on
They would each leave the other's young offspring alone.
No more gobbling them up. But the owl voiced concern:
"I fear that a being so godlike and regal
As you may believe it beneath him to learn
To distinguish my young from all others, Sir Eagle.
So they still won't be safe," wailed the worrying owl.

"Rest your mind, "said the eagle. "Just show them to me
Or describe them minutely so that I can see
How they differ in looks from more commonplace fowl.
I swear I won't touch them."
"Well said, for indeed
In terms of appearance you can't find a breed
To match them. They're pretty and dainty and neat
With such finely formed feathers you'd know them at once,"
Said the owl, quite convinced by parental conceit
This description would save them (poor self-deceived dunce).

Not long after, the owl, having hatched a new brood,
Had to venture away from their nest to find food.
In his absence, the eagle flew by
Just by chance, and his far-seeing eye
Caught a glimpse from his vantage on high
Of a crevice below and therein
Some little birds ugly as sin,
Sour and sad looking, shrieking like Furies.
"Those can't be the owl's offspring," Eagle averred.
"I can crunch them to pieces without any worries."
So he did. He was always a ravenous bird.

When the owl reached his nest all he found were the beaks
And the feet of his darlings. Sobbing "Alas!"

He called on the gods and implored them with shrieks
To punish the villain who'd brought this to pass.
Someone heard him and said "But that villain is you
       Or rather that too common view
       Which holds the members of its race
       Superior in form and face.
Be honest. That portrait you lovingly drew,
       Would anyone else find it true?"

XIX The Lion Going to War

King Lion, deciding to take to the field,
Held a council of war, then dispatched in his name
      His provost marshal to proclaim
      To all the beasts that each must wield
      His special gifts. The elephant
      Must haul provisions on his back,
      The bear defend against attack
      His fellows in the regiment.
The fox could serve as a cunning scout,
The prancing apes provide distraction.
"But the donkeys" someone said "should be mustered out.
They're too heavy and dull to be fit for action.
And the hares are too skittish."
                  "You're wrong," said the king
"For without them my army would not be complete.
The donkey's harsh trumpet will scare off the foe
And cause them to beat out a hasty retreat
While for carrying messages to and fro
The hare's fabled swiftness will prove just the thing."

In truth, a wise monarch can always discover
In the least of his subjects some valuable trait.
      It's knowing how to look them over
      That makes him fit to rule a state.

XX The Bear and the Two Companions

Two companions whose coffers were low
Told a furrier friend that they'd sell
Him the skin of a bear even though
The beast was still living, a minor detail.

This bear, as they told it, was chief of his tribe
And his pelt was so large and so heavy and thick
One could cut two robes from it instead of just one
And the warmth it would yield one could hardly describe.
It would fetch in a fortune, they promised, real quick,
Extolling "their" bear though they hadn't yet done
The one deed to make him theirs, put him to death.
They lauded him more than Dindenaut did his flock
And they promised their friend in the very same breath
That in two days at most they would bring the skin back.

They agreed on a price and set out on their way
And encountered the bear later on that same day.
He rushed out to meet them. The hunters turned pale
As the awful truth struck: There wouldn't be any sale.
To protest the bear owed them was clearly absurd
So the two of them prudently said not a word.
Instead one dashed up to the top of a tree
While the other one froze and lay quiet as death
Not daring to stir or take even one breath
Taking scant comfort from something he'd heard—
         That bears attacked less frequently
         Bodies that neither breathed nor stirred.

And indeed the bear seemed to be fooled by this ruse
But it still was suspicious and with its great paws
It prodded the body and sniffed it as well
         To check its status by its smell.
"It stinks. It's a corpse. There's no reason to stay,"
Said the bear, and he trotted serenely away.

151

Whereupon the first fellow came down from his tree
And ran to his friend and exclaimed with relief
"Thank God you escaped so miraculously
Without the skin, granted, but with no more grief
        Than just your momentary fear.
        But tell me, when he came so near
        I saw him whisper in your ear.
What was his message? What did he say?"

"'Never venture to sell,' he advised strong and clear,
'The skin of a bear you have yet to slay,'"

XXI The Ass Dressed Up in a Lion's Skin

Having wrapped himself in a lion's hide
      An ass evoked such fear
That all the beasts were terrified.
Not even the bravest came near.

Alas for him, his costume slipped;
      His ear's top was disclosed.
      The fraud now being exposed,
Martin the servant came and whipped
      Him back to work while all
Who hadn't seen that telltale ear
Marveled that Martin could commandeer
      A lion to a stall.

There are many fine folk in France today
      To whom this fable applies.
It's in posturing and proud display
      That all their valor lies.

The Hare and the Tortoise

Book VI

I The Shepherd and the Lion
II The Lion and the Hunter

Our fables are not quite what they seem to be.
The simplest of beasts turn out wiser than we.
An unadorned moral is merely a bore;
A tale sneaks its precepts in through the back door.
By such feigning we have to delight as we teach,
A goal that, thank God, I find easy to reach.
The charms of this genre, the wit it engages
Have drawn famous men to it all through the ages;
Their style famously terse and unmarred by excess,
Each poet couldn't have managed with even one word less.
While succinctness earned Phaedrus a measure of blame
Our Aesop was still more adept at that game.
But one man, a Greek, far outdid all the rest
Taking pride in the way his creations expressed
Tale and moral at once in just four lines of verse.
Let the experts decide; was this better or worse?

See how Aesop and he treat a similar theme.
Though the actors may differ, the lesson's the same,
Whether huntsman or shepherd, as you'll presently see
By reading the version created by me.
I'll start out with Aesop but change his design
By adding some touches exclusively mine.

A shepherd, on counting his flock, was distraught
To find some were missing. "The thief must be caught,"
He vowed, and he hurried away to a place
Frequented by wolves, sure that this was the race

Of the culprit he sought. There he took up his stand
Near a cave and some lakes that were spread through the land.
          "Lord Jupiter," the shepherd prayed,
"If you will deliver the rascal to me
          Who dwells in this vicinity
          To show I'm grateful for your aid
          I'll offer up most willingly
          The finest fattest calf I have."

Whereupon there emerged from the mouth of the cave
A fierce roaring lion. The shepherd in shock
Acknowledged "We mortals do not understand
The folly, alas, of the things we demand.
To track down the thief who had ravished my flock
And then see him drowned, I had promised to stay
And to slaughter a calf as an act of thanksgiving.
Oh Lord, just permit me to go on my way
And I'll make it a bull—if I'm still living.

          So Aesop tells it. Now let's go
To his follower's version, given below.
          A swaggering hunter one day found
          That he had lost his finest hound.
          A lion ate it he suspected
          And asked a shepherd to be directed
          To the villain's lair in order to
          Take the revenge that was his due.
          "It's near this mountain," he was told.
          "I know the spot, for from of old
          I'd leave my monthly tribute here,
          One sheep, whereby unvexed by fear,
          I'm free to pasture far and wide
          In the surrounding countryside."

          They'd scarcely finished talking when
          The lion burst forth from his den,
          His claws outstretched. The swaggerer paled.

All his grand schemes for vengeance failed.
"Jupiter, save me please," he cried.
"Show me a place where I can hide."

The true test of courage isn't how
One flirts with dangers that aren't near
But rather that when fierce foes appear
One stands his ground and keeps his vow.

III Phoebus and Boreas

Once in autumn the Sun and the North Wind observed
        A traveler well armed for harsh weather,
For that season's so changeful one's needs are best served
By the utmost precaution. All mixed up together
Come rain and then sunshine, then torrents again.
A rainbow appears, the next minute more rain.
In that season the ancients had well dubbed uncertain
The man knew he would have to keep more than his shirt on.
He was wrapped in a mantle of fabric so stout
It could keep the most inclement elements out. .

"So he thinks he's prepared but he hasn't a clue,"
Said the North Wind, "about what I'm able to do.
When I get really angry and let out a blast,
Of all his stout buttons not one will hold fast
And his cloak will fly off and be blown far away.
That will be a fine spectacle, wouldn't you say?
Shall we bet on it?"
                        Answered the Sun, "Better yet,
I'd like to propose an alternative bet.
Which of us two can more quickly provoke
        That gentleman to shed his cloak?
You go first. In the meantime I'll hide 'neath a cloud."
"Agreed," said the North Wind and took a deep breath
And puffed out his cheeks in the shape of a wreath
        And like a demon roared aloud.
He huffed and he puffed. Everything in his path,
Rooftops and ships' masts alike were laid low
        So fiercely did the North Wind blow
        Just to win the bet he'd made.
But the traveler, a sensible man, wisely stayed
Sequestered away from the force of the storm
        And consequently met no harm
        While his well-made mantle kept him warm.

"Time's up. It's my turn," said the Sun,
  Dispersing the clouds and shining down.
His sultry rays pierced through the traveler's coat;
  In no time he was drenched in sweat
And flung off his coat—though I'd have you know
  The Sun had barely begun to glow.

You can see the moral that's coming of course:
Gentle warmth's more effective than brutal force.

IV Jupiter and the Tenant Farmer

Jove once had a farm that he wanted to let.
He had Mercury announce it, and many folk came
       But the bidding was at best quite tame
       As they saw the land and began to fret.
"It's so wild and forbidding," one farmer cried,
       A verdict echoed on every side.
So the hesitant haggling went on till one man
Who was bold if not wise said "I've thought of a plan.
       Jupiter, I'll farm your land
       Provided that I can command
The weather so that when I call for some rain
Or a dry spell, a breeze, or a blazing hot sun,
Whatever I wish shall be instantly done."

His terms were accepted. A contract was signed
Permitting the farmer, as he was inclined,
To summon now sunshine, now wind, now rain cloud
To his plot alone while the rest of mankind
Accepted whatever the heavens allowed.
At the year's end their harvests and loaded down vines
Proved their luck had been better than his poor designs.

       Viewing this outcome ruefully
       Next year he changed his strategy.
But all his fine tuning of weather and wind
       Made not one difference in the end.
His neighbors once more fared far better than he.
In shame he confessed to the King of the Gods
       How foolishly he'd played the odds.
And was gently received in the hope that he'd see
       That Providence allots our goods
With far more wise forethought than we.

V The Cockerel, the Cat and the Little Mouse

A young mouse, a babe who'd seen nothing as yet,
     Almost met, unawares, a sad end.
He ran to his mother fired up to relate
The adventures he'd had when he traveled beyond
His familiar surroundings. He said "Do you know
I could wander about just as free as a breeze?
     There was no place that I couldn't go.

"And I saw many wonderful things if you please,
     Especially two animals who
Were as unlike each other as day's unlike night.
     The one was so pretty and sweet,
The other so strange that he gave me a fright
     With his harsh voice and huge claws for feet
And a horrible outgrowth of flesh on his head
     And weird arms that allowed him to fly,
And the plumes in his tail like a fan were outspread."
     So it was with his innocent eye
That he painted a picture of—merely—a cock
     But to him some rare alien race.
And he blushed to confess that the terrible shock
     Of meeting that fiend face to face
And hearing the noise that it made when it beat
     Its sides with those strangely formed arms
Was, "Mother, so great that it set off alarms
That even my usual courage couldn't defeat
     And I ran away pale as a sheet.

"And as a result I missed out on the chance
     To meet up with a possible friend,
That other new creature in whose countenance
     Rival features agreeably blend,
A modest demeanor but bright sparkling eyes
     And other traits so like our own,
Velvet fur, pointy ears, a long tail. No surprise

That I wished he'd become better known.
I prepared to approach him but hearing that shriek
    From the other one ruined my plan."

"Just as well," said his mother. "That friend you would seek
    Has been our foe since time began.
        He's a Cat! And his smile
        Is just meant to beguile.
        Had you not run in fear
        You'd be cat food, my dear,
        While the creature you fled
        Gave you no cause for dread.
    Why we sometimes even eat those birds
Whereas cats gobble mice as their chief source of food.
    Looks are deceiving; mark my words
    And beware their feigning attitude.

VI The Fox, the Ape, and the Animals

It's said that when the King of Beasts expired
The animals convened to choose his heir.
They sought no less a prince and so required
Each candidate to prove that he could wear
The crown which had so long been stored away
Kept by a dragon in a hidden chest.
They brought it forth into the light of day
To see on which one's head it fit the best.
Each claimant tried it on but none looked right.
Some heads were much too big and some too small.
The horns on some beasts were a grotesque sight.
It seemed they wouldn't find a king at all.

But then young Ape put on the crown for fun,
Frolicked fantastically, made funny faces,
Jumped through it like a hoop till everyone
Was dazzled by his tricks and his grimaces.
"He's great," they all declared and made him king.
Only the Fox retained a shred of doubt
Though for a while he didn't say a thing
Keeping his reservations unspelled out.

Then he paid his compliments and added "Sire,
I alone of your subjects know the site
Of a treasure trove and if you so desire
I'll show you where since it's the king's by right."
The greedy ape rushed off without delay
To seize his prize before it disappeared.
He fell into a pit upon the way
And Fox, while coming to his rescue, jeered
"You thought to govern others but indeed
You couldn't keep your own base cravings down."
And so Ape was dethroned and all agreed
Few are the creatures fit to wear a crown.

VII The Mule Who Boasted of His Lineage

A mule who belonged to a bishop took pride
        In his noble connections. He'd bray
        Incessantly day after day
In praise of his mother, so pleased that her side
Of the family were horses. He'd boast of her actions,
        Her travels. No deed was so slight
        That it didn't seem grand in his sight
        And he felt that such splendid connections
        Sufficed to ensure that his name
        Would go down in the annals of Fame.

Even serving a doctor he thought much too low.
But time wrought its changes. Grown shabby and old,
To toil in a mill the poor mule had to go.
        "Well, my dad was an ass," he recalled.

        Although misfortune's only boon
        Is to bring a fool back to his senses
        It still is wise if late or soon
        We bless whatever fate dispenses.

VIII The Old Man and the Ass

An old man chanced to spy while out riding his ass
A meadow abounding in acres of grass.
He let the beast loose and it charged through the field
        To seize the pleasures it would yield,
        Wallowing, scratching, rubbing and pawing,
        Gamboling, snorting, grazing and gnawing,
        Picking entire patches clean.
        Then suddenly a threat was seen.
"We'd best clear out," The old man said.
"Why?" asked the reveler, not raising his head.
"Must I bear double burdens to pay for my treat?"
"It's not that," said the man. "Still it's best to take flight."
"Suit yourself," said the ass. "As for me, I don't care
        Whose is the livery I wear.
        You run away. I'll stay right here.
There's no need to flee some imagined disaster.
Why fear a new foe? We've already a master."

IX The Stag and His Reflection

A stag seeing his image reflected
In a pool was enrapt at the sight
Of his antlers. How grand! His delight,
However, was undercut when he inspected
His legs, which were spindly and mean,
A contrast too painfully seen.
"With these antlers my head tops the top of the wood,
But what does that matter," he sighed,
"When the feet which must bear them along are no good?"
So vexed was he he broke down and cried.

In the midst of all this sighing
A bloodhound chanced upon the scene.
No time to ask "What can this mean?"
Through the woods our stag went flying
Or tried to—but his antlers snagged.
Those ornaments of which he'd bragged
Now trapped him and undid the good
His fleet legs, so misunderstood,
Attempted vainly to provide.
Entangled, snared on every side,
Too late he cursed the gift he'd prized
And valued what he'd once despised.

How we overrate beauty and scorn humble worth
Though the former may cause our downfall
As the stag scorned the legs whose speed served him from birth
While his antlers were no good at all.

X The Hare and the Tortoise

Running fast's not enough. One must start off in time
As the tale of Young Hare and Dame Tortoise makes plain.
When she flung the challenge described in this rhyme
Young Hare laughed and answered her, "Are you insane?
      You'll reach the goalpost first, you claim?
      To make a bet like that's just crazy."
      "Crazy or not, Sonny, are you game?
      I may be slow but I'm not lazy."

So it was settled. The stakes were placed
At the end of the course and whoever raced
To the finish line first would get the prize
Though I've no idea of its form or size.

Now the hare was so swift and the course was so short
That he thought it was pointless to start in a hurry.
He could chase packs of dogs here and yonder in sport;
He could browse, take a nap; there was no need to worry.
      Let's leave him basking at his ease
To observe how his rival's measured tread
      And stately progress by degrees,
Making haste slowly, moved her ahead.

Meanwhile in scorn of a triumph so lame,
One that would scarcely redound to his fame,
      The hare resolved for honor's sake
      To give his challenger a break.
Rather than rush to the starting gate
He played around till it got quite late.
Then at last he looked up and beheld with surprise
Dame Tortoise was almost in reach of the prize.
He dashed off like a shot, but that tardy burst
      Of speed was useless. She came in first.

"So," the plodder crowed, "Are you satisfied?
For all your swiftness I won the day
          And let me point out if I may
That I did it while taking my house for the ride."

XI The Donkey and His Masters

A gardener's donkey railed in protest at his fate
That he had to rise before the sun came out.
"Why, the cocks who greet the dawn by comparison sleep late.
Long before them I am made to run about.
And what for? To carry carrots to some crummy market stand.
What a reason to disturb a fellow's rest."

Fate was touched by his complaint and resolved to take a hand
       And give him a new master. So he passed
To a leather worker next. Was the donkey satisfied?
Did he thank Fate for his change in occupation?
No. The stench, the heavy hides, were a new source of vexation.
       "I want my old job back," the ingrate cried.
"There at least I used to snatch a piece of cabbage on the sly
When my boss's head was turned the other way.
Now the only thing I catch is a rap above the eye."
Fate stepped in. He had a new job that same day.

      As a charcoal burner's beast
      Once again he got no rest
Nor did Fate, assaulted by his new lament.
      "This beats all," she fumed. "This ass
      Makes demands that far surpass
The petitions of a hundred kings combined.
He must think that he's the only creature plagued by discontent
As if no other claims were on my mind."

What Fate said, alas, applies just as well to humankind.
We too never are contented with our lot.
Even when the gods deliver the thing for which we've pined,
Once we have it, suddenly it seems it's not
      Quite right. Their only thanks for interceding
      Is a never-ending stream of further pleading.

XII The Sun and the Frogs

When a great monarch married, his subjects were all
    Swept up in a wild drinking spree.
Only Aesop refrained, saying "These poor fools have small
    Occasion for such revelry.
I recall an old tale which describes how the Sun
    Was also intending to wed
But instead of rejoicing, the frogs every one
    Gave voice to a well-founded dread.
'He'll have children, for sure,' said the horrified frogs,
    'And though one Sun may let us survive,
Some half-dozen will dry up our marshes and bogs
    And there won't be one frog left alive.'

With prescience those lowliest beasts could foretell
That the outcome would plunge them straight down into Hell.
    For poor creatures, frogs reason quite well."

XIII The Villager and the Serpent

A villager in days of old,
A kindly man though none too bright,
One winter morning, as he strolled
His grounds, beheld a piteous sight.
A snake lay stretched out in the snow near his shed.
Stiff with cold, crippled up, it was practically dead.

He stooped to retrieve it, then carried it home
With no thought of the turn of events that might come
As the unforeseen cost of a generous deed.
He only saw the serpent's need.
He warmed it near a glowing fire,
Happy to see his guest revive.
But as its numbed senses came alive
So too did its inborn venomous ire.
It uncoiled and it lifted its head as it hissed
And lunged at its savior but luckily missed.

"You ingrate," he cried, full of justified wrath,
"Is this how you thank me for saving your life?
Die then." And flashing a sharp, shining knife,
With two well-placed slashes he hacked it to death.
Head, body, tail, three writhing parts
Struggled in vain to reunite.
The creature got its just deserts
And who would now bewail its plight?

Charity is a noble trait
Yet whom to help's no easy call.
Ingrates deserve no help at all.
A painful death is their proper fate.

171

XIV The Sick Lion and the Fox

A royal decree was promulgated
And sent forth in King Lion's name
To all his vassals. It sadly stated
Their lord was ill, a crying shame.
To cheer him up it called upon
Each tribe to send a delegation,
Promising them they'd all be shown
The utmost in consideration.
A written pledge, it guaranteed
The visitors would have no need
To fear their monarch's tooth or claw.
And so they came; it was the law.

Only the foxes stayed at home
And one of them explained the reason:
"Look at the tracks of those who've come
In all good faith, not fearing treason.
Every one of them leads to the royal den.
Not one of them leads back again.
We thank the king for his gracious promises
But we're bound to show some hesitation
When all who've accepted his invitation
Never emerge from the royal premises."

XV The Bird Catcher, the Hawk and the Lark

Other people's cruelty
We so often cite as our own excuse.
Self-deluded thus, we fail to see
Sparing others may spare us in turn from abuse.

A peasant had planted a mirror intended
To attract little birds which could then be ensnared.
A lark was drawn in. Whereupon there descended
A hawk who'd been circling the skies all prepared
To swoop on some victim. The lark, not yet trapped,
Was still singing gaily when to her dismay
She found her soft body most cruelly gripped
By the claws of the hawk who had seized on his prey.
But even as he plucked her, in turn he was caught,
All entangled himself in the bird catcher's net.
    "Oh spare me," he pleaded in great alarm.
    "I've never done you any harm."

    The man replied "That may be true.
    But how has that little bird hurt you?"

XVI The Horse and the Donkey

In this life we're required to help one another.
    If death should overtake your brother
    His burdens may become your own.
Thus an ass and a horse once were traveling together
And the latter, unencumbered, scorned even to bother
To notice the hardship that made the ass groan,
So heavily loaded he'd surely break down
And perhaps even die well before reaching town.

"Please, won't you just carry a bit of my load?"
The ass humbly pleaded. "I'm not being rude
But surely to take on a bundle or two
Would be nothing more than a trifle to you."

The horse turned him down with a snort and a sneer
All too soon to regret he'd been so cavalier
    For when the ass collapsed and died
    Not only did he have to bear
    Every last bit of the other's gear
    But also one dead donkey's hide.

XVII The Dog Tricked By His Reflection

What fools we mortals be
Chasing shadows all the time.
The examples that I see
Are too numerous to name.

We need only recall the dog Aesop portrayed
Who, seeing his image while crossing a brook,
Dropped the meat he was holding because he mistook
As equally real the reflection it made.
Jumping in to retrieve it, he practically drowned
And although he returned to the shore safe and sound,
He was robbed of the substance as well as the shade.

XVIII The Carter Who Was Stuck in the Mud

A hay wagon driver once found himself stuck
In the mud, and to add to this stroke of bad luck,
The place where it happened was wild and remote.
Have you heard of Quimper? Then I'm sure that you'll note
        That lonely exiles' solitude,
        Far from all dwellings, rough and rude,
Seems expressly designed to drive men to despair.
        God keep us all from landing there!
But that's where he found himself. Needless to say
        He fumed and cursed at this delay
Pouring his fury out now at his horse,
Now at the potholes that hindered his course,
        Now at his wagon, now at his lot,
        Enmired in this hopeless spot.

At last desperation inspired him to call
On that god whose great strength is admired by all.
"Oh Hercules, help me. Your back once sustained
The weight of the heavens. So could you extend
        Just your arm to pull me out of here?"

        From afar the god's voice reached his ear.
"Hercules helps those who don't just complain.
Stir yourself and you won't have invoked me in vain.
Look around at the hurdles impeding your way
        Then take these steps without delay:
Remove from your wheels that cursed plaster and mud
        That smears your axletree with crud.
Use your pickaxe to break up the larger stones
And smooth out the ruts that rattle your bones.
Are you done? Now I'll help you. Just take up your whip."

"I've got it. What's this? My wheels no longer slip.
      Hercules be praised! You've saved the day."
     "If I have, it's by showing you the way.
Don't count on good fairies or daemons or elves.
      The gods help those who help themselves."

XIX The Charlatan

The world has never lacked for charlatans.
        They've been around forever;
        They think themselves so clever
Boasting their ingenuity outruns
All hurdles; they can even outwit Death.
        Their eloquence gives breath
        To marvels. Why one dared
        Proclaim himself prepared
        To take some rustic fool
        And put the clod to school
And guarantee he'd master oratory.
Better yet and reflecting greater glory
        Upon the teacher's name,
        He said he'd do the same
        With a donkey whom he'd teach
        To master human speech
    So brilliantly that down the road
    He'd have his Ph.D. bestowed.

A prince heard his boast and he sent for the man.
"Well, I've got the donkey. Now see if you can
        Make good on your claim."
        "Very well, Sire, I'm game.
        Just advance me my fee
        And in ten years you'll see,
    Your beast will deliver a dissertation
    Sure to win the whole world's admiration.
If not you may hang me in some public square
And invite the whole world to come laugh at me there.
        You can load my textbooks on my back
        And deck me out with donkey's ears."

        "Why sir, to see you on the rack
        I'd gladly wait a dozen years,"
A courtier cried, "and I'm counting on you
To deliver a very fine speech when I do,

178

A speech full of pathos and wisdom as well
Whose burden expanded in drawn-out detail
With examples and precepts, may properly serve
To give thieves the guidance they need and deserve."

"Don't count on it," the other said.
"By then, the prince, myself, the beast,
One of us at the very least,
Or even you will long be dead."

He was right. It's just a sign of folly
To count on living ten years more.
So let's eat and drink, untroubled, jolly,
And leave it to Death to settle the score.

XX Discord

The goddess Discord, having stirred up her peers
And made a fine mess with that apple she tossed,
        Was banished from their heavenly host
        But soon was taken in with cheers
        By humans, who were likewise glad
        To embrace her brother and her dad,
The first christened Hairsplitting Pedants' Disputes,
        His father Fractious Civil Suits.

        Granted, in deigning to settle below
        She recognized where she should go,
Correctly preferring our civilized lands
        To the rude haunts of tribal bands
Who know nothing of law courts or contracts or priests
        And, living no better than savage beasts,
        Accept no gifts from Discord's hands.

In order to find her a proper abode
Where her service, when sought, could be promptly bestowed,
        Fame advertised, and Discord flew
        To do what only she could do,
From a spark of contention creating a blaze
That burned unextinguished for days and days
Till Fame complained that no matter how active
She was, all her efforts proved counterproductive.
        Not a single sponsor could be found;
        No one wanted Discord to hang around.

        "Oh dear," Fame said. "This will never do.
        We've got to find a home where you
        Are welcome on a daily basis."
Her mind sorted through all the possible places.
Convents would have been fine, but much to her regret
        They hadn't been invented yet.
At last light dawned. The right dwelling for Strife
        Was the domicile of man and wife.

XXI The Young Widow

The loss of one's spouse is a matter for sighs
And louder lamenting. Just don't think that will last.
On the swift wings of Time far away sorrow flies
And back come the pleasures of the past.
        A widow once a year's gone by
        Is quite a different person from
        The one consigned to moan and cry
        In the first throes of widowdom.
The latter, caught up in the flush of her grief,
Bids all comrades farewell as she wallows in tears
(Perhaps true, perhaps false) and asserts her belief
She's beyond consolation. But time brings relief
        And now a welcoming smile appears
        When any new acquaintance nears.
Forget those professions of undying woe.
As this fable—and life—show, it just isn't so.

The spouse of a beauty departed this life
Ushered out by the sighs of his grief-stricken wife.
"My darling, just wait. I'll be joining you soon,"
She cried, clutched her breast, and fell into a swoon.
        He left without her anyway.

Now this wife had a father, a sensible man.
        He let these spasms have their day
        And watched as they reduced their sway.
        Then, most discreetly, he began
        To turn her thoughts another way.
"My daughter," he said, "what's the point of this weeping?
It won't bring your man back from where he lies sleeping.
        It's time you turned your pretty head
        To thoughts of life, not of the dead.
        I know that it may take a while
        But one fine day, please God, you'll smile
        And even dream of being re-wed.
Why some handsome young fellow might well seek your hand,

181

Someone dazzlingly different."
                              "You don't understand.
The chaste life of a cloister is all I demand,"
She protested. Her father kept quiet and waited.

In a month came the changes he'd anticipated:
One day a new gown, a new hairstyle the next,
          Her mourning now a mere pretext
          For outfitting herself anew.
          And there were other changes too
          As amorous occasions grew,
Dances and revels and laughter and fun.
          From morn till night our would-be nun
Was plunged as if into the Fountain of Youth
Into pleasures that turned her, to speak the plain truth,
To notions from which her late spouse was excluded.
But her father said nothing and at last she exploded:
"Dear Father, I know you could never be unkind
But something appears to have slipped from your mind.
Where's that handsome young husband you promised you'd find?"

Epilogue

At this point I had better stop.
Pushing on further's a tedious chore.
Rather than squeeze out the final drop
      I've skimmed the cream. I'll add no more.
      Besides I need to take a break
      To catch my breath, regain my stride,
For Cupid, whose claims can't be denied,
      Has summoned me to undertake
      A different task. And for his sake
      I'll pen the story of his bride,
Poor Psyche, whose sufferings at last end in bliss.
My friends urge me on and their warmth may inspire
      New flashes of poetic fire.
      So I'll begin—and ask but this
That the labor of writing this poem may be
      The last pain Love inflicts on me.

Printed in the United States
By Bookmasters